Hear All Creatures!

The Journey of an Animal Communicator

Karen Anderson

Dedicated to Toby and Monroe

Contents

Foreword

This is a new day for you in understanding your animal companions. Within your heart and soul lie the answers that you seek, the understanding that you desire, and the courage and strength that you may need when the time comes to say goodbye to a dear and trusted friend.

My wish is that your life becomes all you want it to be. Follow your dreams and trust yourself. Honor the animals in your life, for they are but a gift from God that we get to take care of for a short time. Your animal companions anxiously await the chance to share their thoughts and feelings with you. Listen with your heart, and you too will hear all creatures.

In most cases, actual names have been used in the book with permission. In others, they have been changed to protect privacy. The stories themselves are taken from actual sessions.

> Peace and abundance,
> Karen Anderson
> www.KarenAnderson.net

1
An Unexpected
Message

Noah

It was a hot summer day in Spokane, Washington, and I was on my way to a Fourth of July barbeque with some friends. It wasn't even noon yet, but it was already sizzling hot. Other than the heat, nothing about that day seemed unusual. Stopping at a grocery store, I picked up a few last-minute items for the party.

I had no idea that my life was about to change forever. With one eye on my watch, I grabbed some snacks and headed for the party.

Earlier that same year, I had begun my path as an animal communicator. My spirit guides came to me during a meditation session and unveiled the plan for me to follow my heart's desire of working with animals. I studied and practiced, and I surrounded myself with every book, tape and CD I could find on the topic. I practiced on every animal I could, asking all my friends for permission to communicate with their animals.

Soon, I was excited and amazed at the information that was coming through. It was fantastic to be able to understand what the animals were thinking and feeling! It was truly a dream come true for me.

For as long as I can remember, I have always loved animals and had them around me. I felt a kinship and a bond with them that exceeded what I felt in most human relationships. I had possessed an ability to communicate with animals as a child, but only at a level of what a seven or eight year-old might understand.

Since my practice sessions relied on input from family and friends, I began to sense for the first time that not everyone was as excited about me communicating with animals as I was. In fact, one of my closest friends at that time became distant and began making hurtful comments about my new skills. These negative comments really upset me, and I began to practice less and less. I became very quiet about my fledgling communication skills.

By the time of that Fourth of July party, I had practically stopped connecting with the animals and really didn't even talk about it anymore. But all that was about to change.

We were sitting in the shade on a deck when the host of the party asked if I wanted to go see the neighbor's wild bird.

Apparently, this lucky little guy had been rescued from the mouth of one her cats, and they were nursing it back to health. Knowing how much I loved animals, and that I knew how to communicate with them, Terri, the next-door neighbor, had invited me over for a look.

Several of us trotted next door. A few moments later, Terri came out with a beautiful white dove on her index finger.

As I listened to Terri explain how she had rescued the bird from those feline jaws, I extended my finger to this quiet, calm little dove. To my amazement, he stepped easily onto my finger without hesitation. He sat perfectly still, even while several children ran through the room, asking to pet him.

"Ask him if he likes his food!" one little boy yelled.

"And if he likes his cage!" another excited little boy added.

The whole family gathered near me to hear what this little dove had to say. Silently, I said my blessing and prayer, and asked his permission to communicate.

To my surprise, the dove cocked his head at me and mentally replied, "I've been expecting you."

"What's he saying, what's he saying?" cried the children, almost in unison.

"You've been expecting me?" I asked him quietly in my mind, a bit surprised.

"Indeed," he said calmly. "The human who talks to animals," he added in a very matter of fact voice. "I've been expecting you. Tell them the food is fine, but please keep the cats away from the cage. I would also like to be higher."

I repeated to the group what the dove said about his food. Terri confirmed that the dove was being kept in a dog crate on the floor, and that the cats could get their paws inside. I wasn't quite sure what he meant by, "I've been expecting you," so I just kept quiet about that.

"He doesn't want the cats near him. Perhaps you can raise his cage," I suggested, returning my attention to the dove. "Where did he come from?" one boy asked.

"From up above," the dove answered quietly

"Did he come from a family? Does he want to go home?" The questions were being fired at me one after the other.

"I come from heaven above. I am here to meet with you. I have been waiting for this moment," he said to me, quietly perched on the end of my index finger.

Suddenly, I felt a rush. Not wind, but something more internal. The family's questions drifted away, and I could hear only the dove as he spoke directly to me.

Looking directly at me, he declared, "I am here to tell you to follow your heart, follow your path, my child. I am here for you, it is your calling. You know it in your heart. You know the right thing to do."

"What's he saying? What's his name?" the questions from the children kept on coming, but I couldn't take my eyes off the dove.

"You have come up against adversity and negativity," he stated.

At that moment, I remembered the hurtful comments I had experienced. Tears poured from my eyes, not tears of pain but of understanding.

"You have been getting away from this lately, haven't you?" The dove asked.

"Well, yes, I have," I answered telepathically. I realized that the recent events of my life were unfolding like a mini movie in my mind. I saw myself from a strange perspective, almost as though I was watching the past happen again. I sensed my own fears and doubts resurfacing, I felt the sting of pain as my friends made rude comments about my communication skills.

"My child, have you ever been touched by the hand of God?" the little white dove asked. I could feel the warmth of his feet flowing down my hand into my arm; it felt peaceful and comforting.

"Well, I don't think so. I think I would remember that," I stammered back, not quite knowing how to answer.

"Consider yourself touched by His hand." He said, "You are a child of God, you know in your heart that you must continue your work. Fear not, my child, it is your purpose in this lifetime."

I stood in total awe for what seemed like an eternity. The children were anxiously awaiting the dove's answers, but I couldn't speak. I didn't know how to tell them that his messages were meant for me.

"Ask him what he wants his name to be," one of the children demanded, getting impatient with me, as I had been silent for too long.

"Tell them I would like a name with dignity," the dove said.

"He would like a name with dignity," I stammered, trying to regain my composure. I would find out later that the family had named him "Noah." He is with them to this day, in his lovely cage, high above the cats.

2
The Early Years

Prince, Kathi, Tony and Karen in 1971

If I were to sum up in one word what it's like to communicate with animals, that word would be "powerful." Anyone who has shared his or her life with an animal, domestic or wild, knows what I'm talking about. There are some animals we just connect with on a higher level. We bond with them on an emotional plane that somehow exceeds even our closest human relationships.

Communicating with animals is fairly simple. We all have this ability.   As a matter of fact, we send messages to and receive messages from our animals each day, whether we know it or not. This book will help you realize your own abilities and take you further down your path to understanding your companion animals. I'll also share some of my most memorable sessions, and tell you what the animals have revealed to me about life, love and even the "Other Side."   Before I do that, I have to tell you how it all happened.

My earliest memory of connecting with an animal was with my first dog, Prince. Prince was a beautiful collie, just like Lassie, except that he was black and white. I could easily connect with Prince on a level that only a six year-old could understand. I simply knew what he was thinking or feeling, what he needed or wanted, and I left it at that. Prince and I would have simple and silly conversations back and forth, all quietly within our own minds. Actually, I thought that everyone could understand what animals were thinking and feeling. It never occurred to me that my relationship with Prince was unique, or that other people couldn't understand an animal's thoughts.

I always wanted to be around animals. My room was covered with stuffed animals, statues of horses, and every book ever written about them. I loved to read about animals and watch any television show about them. I continued to have conversations with the animals until one summer day, many years ago.

When I was about eight years old, I had a horrible experience with a stray cat, which would end my telepathic conversations.

This pretty, orange and white stray was across the street from my house, and I sent him a message to come over and play with me. He was very hesitant at first, and it took me some time to convince him that I was not going to harm him. When the cat finally crossed the street, a car struck and killed him right before my eyes!

Needless to say, I was horrified. I blamed myself. I was completely devastated and, at that moment, I turned my abilities off. Because of me, this poor little kitty was dead. I was determined never do anything to harm an animal again.

Many years later, however, I reconnected with this beautiful cat. I'll share that experience with you later, in Chapter Five.

As the years went by, I forgot about talking with animals and let my abilities fade. But I still felt very connected to nature and the animals. They were my first and best friends on this Earth, and they have continued to walk side by side with me as the decades have passed.

The author and one of her first rides

3
The First
Message

Beeza

I was living in the beautiful Rocky Mountains, in the town of Bailey, Colorado. My husband, Daniel, and I had two horses, Patience and Dakota, and a growing family of cats and dogs. I had spent the previous eighteen years working in the mortgage industry, and I was hankering for a career change.

So, after attending the Red Rocks Police Academy, Daniel and I were sworn in as deputies with the Park County Sheriff's Department in August of 2000. I also volunteered with a nonprofit group known as the Friends of Park County Animals (FPCA), and I was eventually elected to the board of directors. I assisted with foster care, animal adoptions and community education.

It was during this time that I experienced some behavioral problems with some of my own cats. There was a litter-box issue, and it was driving me to distraction. A friend suggested that I talk with an animal communicator to help resolve the problem. I had never heard of animal communicators before, but I was desperate. Even though I was skeptical, as cops tend to be, I decided to look into it.

I bought several books on the topic and, once I started reading, I couldn't put them down. I was absorbed by this whole idea of communicating with animals. I couldn't get enough of it. At the same time, I had a déjà vu sensation of knowing how to do this, or having done it as a child. It didn't dawn on me that I really had!

One book contained a directory of animal communicators. One day I got really brave and tried to contact one. I was disappointed to find that the listings were old and that most of the numbers were no longer in service. I did, however, leave three messages and waited anxiously for a return phone call. Finally, after what seemed like years (it was actually only a day or so), I got a response.

The soft-spoken woman who returned my call set up a phone session. I wasn't sure how all of this worked, so I listened closely to her instructions. She lived in California and I was in Colorado, so I was even more amazed when she said she didn't need to be near my animals to communicate with them.

I was electric with excitement! Just hearing my own animal companions' thoughts and feelings was beyond my dreams! The appointment came, and I will never forget the first few words.

"Jake says he loves you very, very much." The communicator said to me.

I just about lost it. I knew my cat Jake loved me, but this different, this was Jake talking to me! The session continued, and we covered the litter-box issues as best we could. I was in awe. The communicator described things that she could have no way of knowing. My cat's personality, his attitude, his likes and dislikes; it was all so unbelievable.

I was hooked!

As the end of the session approached, I scheduled three more readings with some of my other cats. I hung up reluctantly, then ran to tell my husband about the experience.

After those first few sessions, I was determined to learn how to communicate with animals on my own. I practiced so hard that I didn't realize I was actually blocking the messages. It took an urgent message from one of my own cats to finally get through to me.

It was at our home in Bailey when the first message came to me from Beeza, a gorgeous, orange and white male tabby who suffered from many health issues even though he was only about three years old. Beeza would suddenly have strange outbreaks of panic or anxiety. He would bite furiously at his own back, then take off like a bullet down the hallway. His skin would twitch, and he seemed to be running from some mysterious, invisible attacker. The veterinarian was stumped.

Along with his panic attacks, Beeza also suffered from Feline Urinary Syndrome (FUS). Anyone who has ever gone through this with his or her cat knows how frustrating it can be to treat this illness.

One Saturday morning, I walked into the kitchen and saw Beeza lying on the floor. I walked over to the counter to make some coffee and said out loud, "Hi, Beeza-Bee, how are you?" Instantly, I heard the words, "I'm blocked."

The words were in my own voice. I heard them very clearly, as though I had said them myself. But I hadn't. I was barely awake, and my mind was only set on making coffee.

I looked around the room, but no one was there. My husband was still asleep in our bedroom. I looked down at Beeza, and I said out loud, "Did you say that?"

"Yes, I'm blocked!" I again heard the words very clearly and urgently.

I bent down and felt Beeza's bladder, and it seemed full and hard to me. I had just taken him to the clinic the day before, and he'd checked out fine and healthy. Now here he was, blocked again. FUS is extremely dangerous and painful, so I immediately got on the phone to the local vet clinic and called Dr. Joe. His wife, Stephanie, got on the phone. I told her that Beeza was blocked and that he'd need to come in right away.

Stephanie handed the phone to Dr. Joe, who very politely told me that there was no way Beeza could be blocked.

"I just examined him yesterday. He had no crystals or mucus, so I seriously doubt that he's blocked. But you can bring him anyway. It may not be worth your time."

Dr. Joe was a great vet, but this time he was wrong. "I'll be on my way." I said, and out the door I went with Beeza in a cat carrier.

I arrived at the clinic and waited for Dr. Joe to finish with another patient. When he was finished, he waved me into the exam room and we put Beeza on the metal table.

"Well, let's take a look and see what we've got." Dr Joe said, with all the patience in the world. "Hmm, that's strange," he said as he palpated Beeza's bladder. "Let's get him in the back and get this bladder emptied before it bursts!"

Beeza was indeed blocked. Stephanie emptied his bladder. Dr Joe scratched his head and looked at me. "How did you know he was blocked?" he asked.

"I just had a feeling," I said, rather sheepishly. I wasn't ready to tell him that Beeza had told me himself!

4
Translating
Messages

Misty

In my first attempts to receive messages from animals, I would see only a very quick flash of something. Sometimes the animals sent images of their food bowls or favorite toys. It was like getting one piece of a puzzle from them. There were times when the messages were very subtle, hardly whispers. At other times, they were extreme, almost shouts.

Understanding the animals' messages took some detective work. My law enforcement skills came in very handy, as I had to learn to trust my intuition and listen to my inner voice. I spent many nights on patrol by myself, with the nearest backup officer thirty minutes or more away. As a deputy, I learned how to read people very quickly and how to assess a situation fast, since my life sometimes depended on it. These skills helped me to realize what the animals were saying.

Sometimes I would hear a word or part of a sentence, like "OUTSIDE!" or "Tell my mom I'm afraid!"

As I continued to practice, I began to receive more detailed messages. I might feel an overwhelming sense of happiness from them or a feeling of sadness. I began to notice that I could see things, hear things and feel things from them. There were times when I didn't understand what they were sending me, as I had not quite learned how to translate the images. It was a skill that required a lot of practice and patience. Meditation and relaxed breathing exercises allowed the messages to come through more clearly.

Sometimes we put too much pressure on ourselves, and it ends up blocking the messages and muddying the water. Once I was able to relax, breathe and focus, the messages started to flow more clearly.

A perfect example of this happened early in my career. I was practicing communicating with my father-in-law, Edwin Anderson's, standard poodle, Misty. One of the questions I asked Misty was, "What's your favorite treat?" "MEATBALLS!" Misty yelled, very loudly.

"Meatballs?" I asked.

"MEATBALLS!" she yelled again, very excited to be talking about her favorite treat.

That's strange, I thought to myself. I just couldn't see my inlaws feeding Misty a spaghetti and meatball dinner. I proceeded to tell my father-in-law what Misty said.

"Well, I'm sorry to say, but you're wrong, Karen. Misty doesn't eat meatballs. In fact, we don't eat meatballs."

"Oh well," I said, rather deflated, "I guess I was wrong."

It's very upsetting as a beginner to hear that you're delivering the wrong answer. I was so sure that Misty said "meatballs." In fact, she'd yelled it at me. It was about two days later that I got a phone call from Edwin.

"Hey, pal, I need to apologize to you," he said, rather sheepishly.

"About what?" I asked.

"About Misty," he said. "I was home today, sitting at the kitchen counter, having a snack. Misty and I always have an afternoon snack together. As I was slicing a piece of salami for me, I would also slice a piece for Misty. One for me, one for Misty. I was about to toss her another bite, when I looked at the salami and realized, wait a minute….it's made out of meat and round like a ball, MEAT - BALL…MEATBALL!"

From that point on, I realized that the messages may not always be what we think. We tend to humanize our animals' thoughts and feelings. I thought Misty meant meatballs as in spaghetti and meatballs, and so did my father-in-law. We were both wrong! Misty meant salami, but to her it was made out of meat and round like a ball.

Sometimes the animals will put words together to try to explain something to me. It takes a little creativity to figure out what they really mean. A message similar to Misty's came through at my very first public event.

In November 2004, I attended an animal fair at the Spokane County Fairgrounds in Spokane, Washington. I rented a booth and put up a big sign that said, "ANIMAL COMMUNICATOR." I was extremely nervous, and was glad to have my husband, Daniel, with me for moral support.

The local news station broadcast live from the event, and they did an interview with me just before the expo started. With that kind of media coverage, I was busy all day. Since I was too nervous to do any sessions at the expo, Daniel and I were busy making appointments with people for after the show.

Toward the end of the expo, a woman came up to the booth with her dog, a pretty pit-bull mix. She was insistent on having a session with me then and there, and told Daniel that she had driven over an hour and a half just to see me. Neither of us knew this woman. Daniel politely told her that we were only setting appointments and not doing actual sessions at the show. He explained that there are too many distractions, making it difficult for me to hear the messages.

The woman persisted.

Daniel glanced at me with a "What do I do now?" look. For some reason, I waved the woman over to the back of my booth and asked her to sit down for a session.

Her name was Lisa. Her beautiful pit-bull was named Sara. Lisa started right off by telling me that she was very skeptical about this whole process. She didn't even know if she believed in "all this."

I told her I completely understood, as I had once been skeptical myself. I asked Lisa what she wanted me to find out from Sara, who sat obediently at Lisa's side, fixated on the wiener dog races that were still going on in the complex.

"I don't know," Lisa announced nervously. "Ask her if she has any messages for me."

"Okay," I said. "This will just take a minute."

I connected with the dog, and the first thing Sara said to me was, "night trauma."

"Sara is telling me about something called 'night trauma.' Do you know what this means?"

"No," Lisa responded. "I don't think so."

Again Sara told me to say 'night trauma.'

"She's telling me to say night trauma," I persisted. "Is there something going on at night with Sara?"

I knew this had to be important for the dog to keep sending the message.

"Uh, no. Not that I can think of. Doesn't she need to be looking at you?" Lisa asked, still skeptical.

"No," I answered. "She's just fine."

The muscular brown and white dog continued to sit with her back toward me, watching the little dogs racing back and forth.

"So if there's nothing going on at night with your dog, how about with you?" I asked Lisa, her eyes widening like big saucers. "Is there something going on with you at night?"

"With me? Uh, yeah," she said slowly. "I've, uh, had some trouble sleeping lately. Sara gets up with me at night when I can't sleep."

"Interesting," I said out loud, but mostly to myself. Having learned that animals will sometimes put words together to get me to say something, I noted that Sara didn't say "trouble sleeping." She said "night trauma." But in my mind, it was pretty much the same thing.

"Well, Sara is worried about you because of this night trauma," I told her. "She says you're making yourself sick and upset. Do
you know what she's talking about?"
Lisa just stared at me now. Her eyes filled with tears.

"She's also telling me to tell you to stop doubting." I continued on as the messages from Sara were still coming through. Sara was intently watching the wiener dog races, which were a popular event at the expo. Spectators were cheering and screaming as excited little dogs ran back and forth. I looked up at Lisa, whose eyes were now about the size of silver dollars.

"I'm not sure what this is, but Sara is telling me there is this 'BIG THING that you are doubting,' I'm supposed to tell you to stop doubting this BIG THING. Again, I don't know what it is, but she says, 'tell her to stop doubting, stop doubting.'"

I made a gesture with my hands and outlined a "big thing" in the air in front of me as Sara kept telling me to say this.

Lisa started to cry hysterically, sobbing and reaching for a tissue. I had no idea what was happening, so I just waited until she calmed down.

When she regained her composure, Lisa asked, "How did you know that?" She wiped away her tears and blew her nose.

"How did I know what?" I asked. I still had no idea what she was talking about.

"I have been doubting God. I've been doubting the existence of God, and I have been losing sleep over it. How did you know that?" She was still crying.

Through her tears, Lisa said, "There was no way you could have known that. Only my good friends know. They've sent their pastors and ministers to my house to talk to me about God, and the existence of God. I don't believe them; I don't believe what they say. There is no way you could have known that!" She blew her nose again, still mystified and a little stunned. "Sara told me," I answered quietly. "She's worried about you. She loves you."

Lisa sat there trembling for a while, unable to move, unable to speak. Daniel and I just let her sit until she was ready to go. The whole session had all of us a little shaken.

"I guess I owe you an apology," Lisa mumbled as she gathered her belongings. "That was amazing. I don't know what to say." "No apology needed," I said with a smile and a big hug.

"I guess I didn't realize that I was causing Sara to be upset, too. I never meant for that to happen."

Our animals don't always understand what we are upset about. They just know we're worried, and they understand enough to be concerned for us. Sara told me it was something big that was upsetting her mom. I just hadn't realized how big it was!

That wasn't the only difficult-to-understand message that I've had to deal with.

Diamond Encrusted

I was speaking in Seattle, Washington, when a woman in the front row handed me a picture of her cat, Lexi. I had learned to communicate with animals by using just a photo or description. The woman explained that Lexi had recently passed away. Her pain was obvious as tears filled her eyes. Lexi had been with her for nearly eighteen years, and they had shared a lifetime together, including the woman's two divorces.

I connected with Lexi immediately. The woman's eyes filled with tears as I told her that Lexi sent her love to her momma and that she missed her "shiny, round thing. It looks diamond encrusted to me, very shiny, very sparkly. Do you know what this is?" I asked the teary-eyed woman.

"No," she shook her head. "I don't know. Lexi had a collar, but it wasn't shiny, it was stretchy. I'm not sure what that is."

Her sad voice trailed off. It was only a few days after that event that I received a jubilant e-mail telling me the "shiny, diamond encrusted thing" was none other than an aluminium foil ball! In the e-mail, she explained how she and Lexi had played with a foil ball, and that it was Lexi's favorite game! How could she have forgotten that? From Lexi's perspective, I could see how a foil ball could look shiny, sparkly and diamond encrusted.

Then there was the message in which one letter made a big difference.

Lost in Translation

At an event in Santa Monica, California, a lovely retired couple came to see me for a session with their little dog, Casanova. Nova, as they called him, was a three year-old Maltese, and he was just adorable. The photos they brought showed a happy little dog.

They sat down and shared with me only his name and age. I connected immediately with Nova, and he rambled on and on about his life.

He immediately announced, "I love my mom, I love my dad, I love my treats, I love my bed, I love my toys, I love my walks, I love my life!"

Wow, what a happy little guy! His "mom and dad" listened intently to every word he said, they adored him as much as he adored them. There were big smiles all around. They couldn't have been happier to hear such loving things from their sweet little boy.

Toward the end of the session, I asked Nova to tell me something special that only his mom and dad knew. He thought for a moment and said, "Tell them they SMELL to me."

"They smell to you?" I repeated quietly in my head. Oh no, I thought to myself, how in the world am I going to tell this perfectly delightful couple that their beloved little dog thinks they smell? Oh, this is not good, I thought, trying to figure out a way to get out of this one.

I never censor the messages. I tell my clients exactly what I get. So now I was about to contradict myself, or so I thought. Luckily, I went back to Nova and asked, "Did you say your mom and dad SMELL to you?"

"No!" he answered. " I said they SPELL to me, like R-I-D-E and W-A-L-K and O-U-T!" and he proceeded to actually spell out the words, "ride," "walk" and "out."

I looked at the couple and asked, "Do you spell to your dog?" With eyes wide, they looked at each other and started to laugh. "Yes, we do spell to him. He's so smart that we have to spell out the words so he doesn't know what we're saying!"

As everyone was laughing, the little dog added in the background, "Tell them I still know what they are saying, I still know what they are saying."

One letter can make a very big difference indeed.

As Nova showed me, animals are quite capable of knowing much more than what their favorite treat is or their what their food bowl looks like. In the next chapter, you will be amazed at the detailed information the animals have shared with me.

5

Intelligent, Spiritual Beings

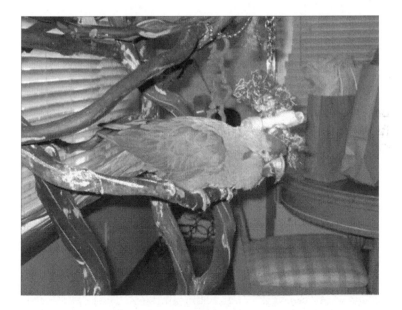

Shamrock

What do our animals know? A lot more than you probably realize. They are intelligent, spiritual beings and have a very wide range of emotions, just like humans. Their messages range from simple accounts of their daily lives to astounding words of philosophical wisdom.

Shamrock, a red fronted macaw, announced during a session with his mom, Fran, that, "The truer we are to ourselves, the more Godlike we become." I couldn't agree more.

Animals are excellent at manipulating their environments or their humans to get what they want. They plot and plan, and some have quite a sense of humor.

Reggie, an orange-and-white male tabby from Florida, thought he would send a wind-up toy across my field of vision instead of answering his mom's questions. It looked like a little cartoon mouse that went back and forth, squeaking across my mind's eye.

"Oh, he's quite the comedian," his mom, Heidi, said as I explained what I saw. "He's always up to some kind of prank. He loves to hide behind the curtains, then jump out and scare me as I come walking down the hall."

Reggie enjoyed all the attention and had a big smile on his face.

Along with fun and happy feelings, animals also experience death and loss in many of the same ways we do. They grieve just as humans grieve when loved ones die. While some animals seem to know that another animal has left the Earth-plane and continued his or her journey into the spirit world, others are at a loss.

"What happened to Roxi?" a sad and depressed cockatiel named Sam asked me. Roxi was his beloved mate and companion for nearly ten years and had recently died of pneumonia.

"Roxi went to the spirit world to continue her journey," I explained to the sad little bird. Sam's worried dad, Steve, had called me because Sam had stopped eating.

"What can your dad do to help you, Sam?" I asked.

"I don't know," he sighed. "It just hurts in my heart."

"Would you like to have a picture of Roxi near you?" I asked, trying to think of something that would make this little bird feel better.

"It won't be the same, but I'll try that," the small voice barely came through.

Steve put Roxi's picture next to Sam's cage, and within hours Sam started to improve and be more like himself again. When I checked with him later, Sam said, "I know it's not Roxi, but it makes me feel good in my heart to see her again."

Tell your animals what happened if someone dies suddenly. They will understand the images that form in your mind as you speak.

Animals understand that we have jobs, and they often send me images of what their humans do for a living. Spartacus, a German shorthaired pointer from Arizona, sent me the image of a nurse's uniform, telling me that his mom was "gone too much and needed to polish her white shoes."

His mom, Teresa, is an emergency room nurse and often worked long, back-to-back shifts. She also admitted that her shoes definitely needed some polishing.

Sometimes animals show me papers stacked all over a desk, or they tell me their humans work too hard and need to have more fun in life.

"Will you tell them I need more time with them?" Sweet Pea, a Springer spaniel, pleaded, "all they do is look at paper all day."

Sweet Pea's mom and dad, Rhonda and John, were in the middle of remodeling their kitchen. Blueprints, paperwork and contractors had taken over their lives. Once they heard Sweet Pea's messages, they made sure there were plenty of walks through the park and playtime with her.

It has long been known that animals help heal our pain and can often take on our ailments or medical issues. They also have the unique ability to discuss the health issues of their humans. There are many times when I'll get a medical reference during a session only to find out that it's the human with that medical condition, not the animal. I may feel pain in my lower back only to find out that the human suffers from lower back pain.

I was lecturing to a group of horse enthusiasts when a woman in the crowd asked if I could deliver a message from her horse, Galileo. I immediately went to my knees and said, "I have a knee issue coming up here, there is pain in the knees, and it's quite intense."

Galileo heard his human mom complaining about the pain in her knees during rides. It turned out that his mom did indeed suffer from two bad knees.

A three year-old Shih Tzu named Binky announced to me, "I have cancer!" very excitedly.

"You do?" I responded, "Do you know what cancer is?"

"No," he replied, "but I get to go to lots of places with my mom so they can look at my cancer!"

Binky's mom confirmed that she took him to every specialist she could find to evaluate Binky's cancer and future surgery. After several weeks, I heard back that Binky was alive, well and cancer-free.

Animals can pick up on terms that we or their veterinarians use to describe their own health issues. They may not know exactly what the condition is, but they know they have it. Animals get very creative, and they come up with their own descriptive language at times.

"Tell mom I need more marshmallow time," a cat named Beep said to me one day.

Her human mom, Vicki, laughed and knew exactly what he was talking about. Beep described their quiet moments, cuddling together on the sofa, with him "making biscuits" in Vicki's lap, a sweet, precious time for both of them.

Big Sneeze

A beautiful koi named Big Sneeze told me, "The wisdom we all seek lies within our own hearts. Inner beauty knows no limits, inner peace no boundaries. The lines between human and animal sometimes blur as the soul progresses and realizes its full potential."

Animals are naturally very in tune with the Earth, seasons, nature and lunar cycles. They often share with me that there is a "big trip" coming up, "many moons from now," meaning many full moons or months from now. They know that a full moon is equal to one month. They also understand the dark of night and the light of day.

"I will be gone for three dark nights," I tell my animals before a trip. It lets them know I will be back and when to expect me. Many animals with separation anxiety can be helped by simply telling them that you will be back, then picture yourself coming back through the door at the appropriate time.

Animals also have the ability to tell time or have a very accurate sense of timing. I have an agreement with some of my outdoor cats to be sure to be home by a certain time, and there they are waiting for me at the door at our pre-arranged time.

"You're late," my big boy, Bandit, said one day.

"I know. I'm sorry, Bandit. Did you miss me?" I asked, trying to change the subject.

"You don't like it when we're late." He said as he swished past me through the door. He was absolutely right.

There is almost no limit to the amount of knowledge and information our animals can share about themselves, the planet, health issues, or their own spiritual paths. Animals are very excited about sharing their world with us, with very few exceptions. Sometimes it's the little things that mean the most, as you'll find out in this next story.

Apples in the air

I believe that horses are some of the most spiritual beings on this planet. The connection between horse and rider goes beyond the spoken word. Horses are extremely sensitive creatures and capable of so much more than we may realize.

Through the many sessions I have had with horses over the years, I have found their instincts to be their strongest motivators. Often misunderstood, with their instincts viewed as behavioral problems, horses are just doing what horses do. They tell me they see their humans as part of their herd and relate to them in the same way they would relate to other horses.

Developing a mutual respect, which includes showing them their limits and boundaries, sets the stage for a harmonious relationship.

Be very clear when you spend time with your horse. These amazing creatures can feel a mosquito land on their flanks. Imagine what it feels like to have all of our weight on their backs.

Horses also talk about their food, what they like or dislike. Some are very specific, like Toby, a seventeen year-old Morgan gelding.

"My favorite treat is a banana," Toby told me, showing me the color and shape.

His human confirmed that he often carries a banana in his backpack on long rides. Although the horse didn't eat the banana, he saw how much his human enjoyed it and assumed he would like it too.

Other horses have told me that their bits pinch their mouths or their saddles cause them pain or discomfort. I've heard from many horses that have recurring back pain and can often benefit from chiropractic adjustments. All of that considered, the most common response I hear from horses is that we send them too many messages, and they are overwhelmed with incoming information.

They tell me they generally try to do what their humans ask, but the messages are so confusing they sometimes get frustrated and ignore them all.

Be aware of your body language, your movements, shifting weight in the saddle, your speech, your tone. Pay attention to the thoughts running through your mind. You're sending your horse messages all the time, and he or she is trying to listen.

Horses often respond to us with tempered frustration, a swish of a tail, a cock of the ear, a flinch or skin quiver. These are all messages from our horses. We need to pay attention and listen to them as well.

One horse told me that his mom only listens to him with "her ears half open."

When I asked what he meant, he explained that during their rides his mom, "shuts down my words, and I can't get through to her."

I think many of us realize that we need to listen to our horses more. We need to watch their body language and observe their moods. It's very common to think the worst-case scenario will happen as we begin a ride or a training session with our horses. Then, sure enough, they do exactly what we don't want them to do.

Little did we know that we sent our horses an exact image of what we were hoping to avoid.

Think in positives with your horse. Think of what the completed task looks like or how the horse looks going over the jump smoothly. Be aware that your horse is reading your thoughts and the images in your mind the whole time. Send him or her clear and precise messages of what you want, not what you don't want.

Laurie called me because she wanted to check in with her two Icelandic horses, Lodur and Skjoni (pronounced lo-der and skeeonee).

When I connected with Lodur, he delivered many meaningful messages for Laurie. He told me that he was the "special one," and Laurie confirmed that she often called him "my special one."

Laurie asked Lodur which one of his two bits he preferred, his regular bridle or the bitless bridle, which is a headstall without the bit, or metal part, that goes inside the mouth. Lodur preferred the bitless bridle. The only problem was that Laurie couldn't get him to stop on command when he wore this bridle.

When I asked Lodur about this, he explained that he was "tired of their boring walk-abouts" and wanted to run more and be free. Laurie confirmed that she made him walk during most of their rides as she was not confident that he would stop on command.

Laurie and I worked out a deal with Lodur. She would use the bitless bridle, but he had to listen to her commands. Lodur shut down briefly when I asked if he was up to this challenge, but soon came back with his full attention. Lodur agreed to behave himself with the bitless bridle, and to this day, some two years later as I write this, Laurie confirms that Lodur stops on a dime every time.

When I connected with Laurie's other horse, Skjoni, he told me how upset he was about being penned up in his stall.

"Tell her I feel tied or I can't move around, and I don't like this," Skjoni explained.

Laurie confirmed that Skjoni was on stall rest from a recent scuffle with Lodur, and had to be confined until his wounds healed. After many insightful messages, the session drew to an end.

I asked Skjoni if there was something special or important I could tell his mom.

He answered, "Tell her apples in the air." I repeated that sentence to Laurie.

Lodur

Skjoni

"I'm supposed to say, apples in the air, apples in the air. What does that mean?" I inquired.

Laurie laughed in delight and explained that her neighbor drives by her horses in his truck, rolls down the window, then tosses apples through the air into their corral.

Apples in the air.

You just never know what animals will say. Their answers can be very interesting, but as you'll read in the next story, sometimes it's the question that surprises me.

Fear

During a session, I'm usually the one asking the questions. One day, a female boa constrictor named Azira turned the tables on me. Azira had stopped eating, and I was checking with her to see what might be causing her lack of appetite. Although it's normal for snakes to go for a period of time without eating, Azira was long overdue for a meal.

"What is this thing you humans call fear?" she asked, ignoring my questions about food.

I found myself grasping at how to answer this penetrating question. I suddenly felt responsible for all the humans who may have reacted to her in fear. It was a difficult question, so I thought carefully about her perspective before I answered.

"Well, my friend," I answered very slowly, "sometimes humans fear what they don't understand. Once there is an understanding, the fear begins to subside. You are a gorgeous, intelligent soul, and there are many who honor and respect you. Perhaps you will inspire those who don't understand you to realize and face their own fears."

"Perhaps," she said, rather discouraged. "I cannot understand the human thought."

I felt oddly inadequate at that moment. Then she quickly changed the subject.

"Tell them I need to feel the warmth of the sun on a rock before I can eat again." She announced, finally acknowledging my earlier questions.

Apparently, Azira's pen had several tree limbs in it but no rocks. Once a heated rock was placed inside her pen, she began to eat again. Animals are very attuned to their surroundings, and it's always best to provide the most natural setting possible.

Sometimes animals share strange and seemingly insignificant little tidbits of information, or show me odd things that are going on in their daily lives.

Ashley, a beautiful gray cat in California, showed me strange, geometric lines going across the kitchen floor.

"What is this?" I asked Ashley.

"I don't know," she answered. "It's messy."

Ashley's mom, Ursula, confirmed that she was in the process of having the grout removed from the tile on her kitchen floor. The workers had to remove the old grout and put new grout in. It was a very messy job. The tiles created a geometric, diagonal pattern on the kitchen floor.

For whatever reason, this messy, noisy event was important enough for Ashley to bring up during her session.

Ashley

I also asked Ashley where she liked to sleep. She showed me a waffle-weave pattern. I explained the pattern to Ashley's mom, yet Ursula insisted that was incorrect.

"No, Ashley likes to sleep under the TV cabinet, and it's carpeted under there." Ursula replied.

It was later that night that I got a call from Ursula telling me I was indeed right. When she headed to bed that night, Ashley had climbed onto her normal spot to settle on top of the duvet cover.

(A duvet cover is similar to a bedspread.) Ursula looked down as she was saying goodnight to Ashley, and she noticed that the duvet cover had a raised, waffle-weave pattern to it.

Ashley knew what she liked. She was a very detail-oriented cat.

Along with patterns, animals also can see color. There seems to be quite a debate among scientists about whether this is true. In my experience, animals describe all kinds of colors and patterns.

"Tell her I like the purple toy the best," said Jovi, Ursula's new, blue-eyed rag doll kitten.

Ursula confirmed that, out of all his toys, Jovi liked the purplefeathered toy the best.

So the debate rages on.

I know a rather determined little Jack Russell terrier named Stella who told me that her favorite treat was pretzels. I knew first hand that Stella didn't like pretzels because I visited her often while I was on duty with the sheriff's office. I offered

Stella

pretzels to her from time to time, and she would just stare at them in disgust.

Then, right after she told me her favorite treat was pretzels, she gobbled them up like raw meat, for that one day. After that, she never ate them again. Stella still holds down her very important position as head of security at the largest gun store in Bailey, Colorado.

Although animals are very much in the moment, they do acknowledge the past and will often share detailed experiences with me about their former humans, former homes and sometimes, their past lives.

One of the most memorable past-life experiences I heard was with a little poodle mix named Otis. Otis was very chatty, and he told me all about his past lives. He showed me many of his adventures, from early Egypt to the American pioneer days.

"Which one was your favorite?" I asked

"When I was an octopus!" he answered excitedly.

"An octopus?" I asked, rather surprised and trying to keep my composure.

"Yes, an octopus," he stated, in a very matter of fact way. "I see. Well, when you were an octopus, where did you live?" I asked, not quite knowing how to respond to that one.

"IN THE SEA!" he answered in a very stern voice. He was obviously a bit annoyed with me for not knowing where an octopus would live. Even a ninny would know that.

Most of my spiritual beliefs are based on what the animals have shared with me over the years. I really didn't believe in past lives or give reincarnation much thought until I started hearing about all the experiences from the animals. Some discuss their past in great detail, while others don't show much interest in it. Every animal is unique.

Animals have also told me that they reincarnate and can choose to come back to us several times during our lifetime. From what they tell me, most animals return as the same species, but they do have the ability to change if they so desire. For instance, most cats tend to have past lives as cats, but they have also shown me that they have had past lives as a bears, birds and dogs. Animals have life lessons to learn just as humans do, and they can choose to come back to us many times to complete these lessons.

If you would like your animal friends to return to you in this lifetime, just ask them to do so. If it is so written in their spiritual paths, they will most likely come back to you again and again. When they do come back, you may only get one chance to recognize your long-lost friends. Sometimes you may catch a glimpse of a habit or personality trait that your previous animal friend had. Other animals make it very obvious that they have returned to you.

One beautiful Siamese cat, Penny, returned to her human reincarnated as a new kitten. This kitten was an unexpected delight that showed up on her doorstep one day. The woman who found her, Nancy, had lost Penny several years earlier to cancer. Nancy always asked Penny to return to her in her thoughts and prayers. When this little kitten showed up, Nancy was amazed at how many similarities she had to Penny. But the final, discerning moment was when the kitten jumped up on her counter one morning and ate her cantaloupe.

This was something that Penny had done in the past. We later confirmed through a session that the kitten was indeed Penny, returning to Nancy for another enchanted lifetime.

I had a personal experience with reincarnation that I mention in Chapter One. When I was about eight years old, you may recall, I was in my front yard, mentally calling to an orangeand-white stray cat across the street. I invited him to come over and play with me. After what seemed like forever, the cat made a dash toward the street. Then, right before my eyes, a car came out of nowhere and killed the cat, with a loud thud. I watched, horrified, as his twisted body went limp on the asphalt.

At that devastating moment, I swore I would never try to communicate with an animal again. It was my fault that this beautiful creature died; I had called him across the street to meet his death.

More than thirty-five years passed, and I carried this burden of guilt with me. I believe that the reason I got so involved with cat rescue as an adult was because of this one incident. I couldn't save that cat, but I could save others.

Recently, I was discussing this story with a friend, who very nonchalantly suggested, "Why don't you connect with that cat in the spirit world and find out why that happened?"

It seemed so obvious, but I just didn't want to go there. It was such a horrible experience that opening up that old wound was the last thing I wanted to do. However, everything I've experienced from animals who have crossed over to the spirit world has been all about forgiveness, love and compassion. It took me a while to gather the nerve to do it, but I finally connected with that same cat who had died so many years before.

I called to him, as I remembered him, the orange-and-white tabby from long ago. I asked the angels to bring his energy to me. As his energy began to come through to me, I felt a strange sense of familiarity. I wasn't quite sure why. I explained to him how very sorry I was for having called to him all those years ago, and how horrified I was that he was killed because of my actions. The tears poured down my face as I offered him one apology after another.

"My child," he said softly. "There is no need for sorrow, no need for blame. It was I who decided to leave the Earth at that moment. It was not your decision to make. It was not your burden to carry."

Not sure what he meant, I said, "Please know that I would never do anything to cause any pain or harm to any animal, and I have been wracked with guilt and pain over what happened so many years ago. Can you ever forgive me? Why did it have to be this way?"

"So I could return to you once again and keep you on your path to glory and the Divine," he answered somberly.
"Can you explain?" I asked, still unsure of his message.

"My dear child, let me show you as I am today," and with that he flashed an image of himself as he is now. I was speechless, I couldn't move. I just sat there and held my breath. I couldn't believe what I was seeing.

There, before my eyes, was the white dove Noah (whose story is recounted in Chapter One)!

"I was sent to you early in your life to help you on your path, your destiny, to allow you to learn and to grow in your work with the animals. I left this Earth at that exact moment so I could return to you later in this lifetime to keep you focused and pointed in the right direction. It was meant to be this way. The

Universe has played out as it should."

In one moment, thirty-five years of grief and guilt melted away with my tears. It all made such perfect sense now. It was meant to be.

The animals have been there for me during the good times, bad times and everything in between. Along with helping us on our journeys through this lifetime, the animals are also here to teach us other lessons, like patience and perseverance, as the next chapter reveals.

6
Behavior Problems: The Litter Box Chronicles

Ricki Tik

I can't start this chapter without talking about the numerous calls I get about litter box use, or should I say litter box misuse. This is by far the biggest complaint of those with indoor cats, especially in multi-cat households.

Anyone who has experienced a litter box problem knows the frustration when a cat refuses to use the litter box. There are as many reasons why cats won't use their litter boxes as there are cats.

Some basic reasons are they don't like the box itself, either covered or uncovered. They don't like the litter: Scented litter can be offensive to a cat's powerful sense of smell. They don't like the location of the litter box. Placing a litter box near the laundry room is a recipe for disaster that should be avoided if at all possible.

Cats prefer quiet locations where interruptions are kept to a minimum. They also don't like to travel all the way to the farthest room in the basement. Many cats have told me that the litter box is just too far away. A litter box in the basement may seem like a good idea, but some elderly cats don't like to travel up and down stairs. Other cats have told me they don't like the litter in their box. Some cats prefer tiny, soft litter, while others like chunky litter. And the biggest reason indoor cats don't use their litter boxes is because they don't want to use one that other cats use.

Medical conditions may also cause litter box issues. A thorough check by a veterinarian will eliminate a possible bladder infection, crystals or other problem that alters a cat's litter box routine. In a multi-cat household, the golden rule is: one box per cat, plus one box.

If your vet check doesn't reveal any health issues, I suggest you take a look at your overall situation at home. Changes in your schedule add stress to many cats and may prompt a litter box problem. A new job, a new baby, a new animal, divorce, any type of stress-related situation can cause a happy cat to stop using the litter box.

Most of the time, they're trying to tell you something. Something is out of balance or upsetting them. In the next story, though, it was a matter of personal hygiene.

Tummy's Tale

Tummy was a gorgeous, nine year-old female calico cat from Texas. Her fur was silky and fabulous, and she had beautiful yellow-green eyes. Her mom, Sharon, contacted me to see if I could figure out why Tummy stopped using her litter box.

Sharon explained that Tummy would use her bathtub as a litter box, and that she had tried everything to appease the cat. Sharon purchased a new litter box with a covered lid. She tried new, unscented litter. She put a night-light on so Tummy could see it in the dark, and gave her lots of praise when she went near the litter box. Sharon did many things right.

As I connected with Tummy, she described a very nice life with her mom, whom she loved very much, and all of her favorite things, including toys, places to lounge, and a big window where she could watch the birds.

When I asked her about her litter box, she said, "Oh, that disgusting thing!" and put her nose up in the air.

Many cats won't use dirty litter boxes, but Sharon assured me that she kept Tummy's litter box immaculate.

"Oh no, its clean," Sharon responded. "She never uses it, so there's nothing in it except clean litter!"

When I asked Tummy why she wouldn't use the box, she explained that she felt it was "too dirty" for her, even though it was spotless. Tummy felt the litter left a powdery residue on her fabulous fur. She didn't want to get any of that on her, so she simply went into the bathtub!

I asked Tummy if she would consider using the litter box if there was no litter in it at all. Tummy thought about it for a moment, then said, "Okay, tell mom I'll do my best."

I told Sharon about Tummy's opinion on the litter residue, and that she was open to trying an empty box. I advised Sharon to start by putting an empty litter box in the bathtub where Tummy was currently going. Then, each week, move the box a little closer to where she ultimately wanted it to be.

It worked! Sharon sent me a note to say that Tummy immediately went into the new empty box and has done so ever since. She said she was able to slowly move the box out of the bathtub and into a nice quiet corner of the bathroom.

Finding a solution that fits your cat's needs is always the best approach. Punishing your cat will only teach him or her to fear you. It may take a little creativity, patience and persistence. Just be willing to try different options.

In the next story, I was asked to tell a cat *not* to use the litter box. Now I'd heard everything!

A Bizarre Litter Box Story

Ricki Tik is a gorgeous, black-and-white cat with a paralysis known as cerebellar hypoplasia in his hind legs. This condition affects an animal's movements, causing tremors and unusual, jerky movements. His mom and caretaker, Jamie, is a dear friend of mine in Idaho. Jamie cares for many unwanted, abandoned or special-needs cats. Ricki Tik is one of the latter.

I've been contacted many times for litter box problems, but this one was unlike any other. Jamie wanted me to tell Ricki Tik not to use the litter box. With the jerky movements caused by his paralysis, Ricki Tik made a huge mess as he struggled around in the litter box, creating even more clean-up for Jamie. This was a new one on me.

When I explained to Ricki Tik that his mom wanted him to use the towel for his elimination needs, Ricki Tik responded in a surprising manner. He very politely told me that he was very proud of himself for "finally making it into the big box" like the other kitties. It had taken a long time for him to accomplish this.

After hearing this, Jamie decided to let him make a big mess after all. Now that he has the hang of it, Jamie reports that Ricki Tik is very good in the box and hardly makes a mess at all!

The Fearful Horse

Lorna called me about her nervous quarter horse, Jack. Jack's spooky behavior was frustrating Lorna during their rides, and she was unsure what to do about it.

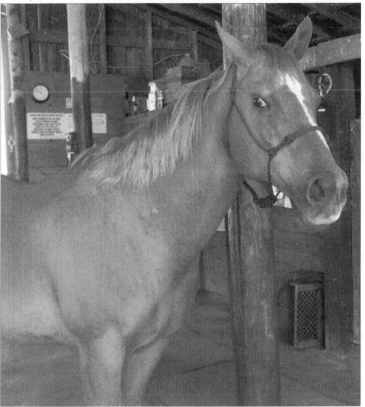

Jack

When I connected with Jack, he shared with me some very unpleasant experiences from the past. Former owners had not been kind to him, causing him to develop his jumpy, nervous behavior. Jack made me feel like every ride with Lorna was like dodging hidden tigers in the grass, ready to pounce.

As with many horses, Jack was unsure if he was going to be staying with his current owner. I explained to Jack that this was his "forever home" and that Lorna would be with him until it was time to pass into the spirit world. I convinced Jack that Lorna would never harm him or lead him into any dangerous situations. I advised Jack to trust Lorna and to let her help him move forward into a happier existence.

Once I communicated with Jack, I turned my attention to Lorna. It seemed as though they were playing into each other's hands. Lorna would anticipate Jack's behavior, and her anxiety would build as their rides progressed. Jack sensed her nervousness, and he got even more nervous. I explained to Lorna that she needed to let go of any negative feelings and "wipe the slate clean" with Jack. She needed to be confident in her abilities and confident that Jack would do exactly what she wanted him to do. I told Lorna that every time she sensed Jack slipping into his old behavior, to "jiggle the reins" and get his attention back on her instead of the scary world.

Once she put this into practice, the change was remarkable. Here's what Lorna wrote:

Karen-

I'm so excited I had to tell you about a ride I had on Jack. It was the best ride ever since having him. I took all of your good advice and spoke to him about letting go the past then took charge and rode him for the first time ever in this other arena area - no fencing. I have been putting off riding him there due to his spooky mentality.

I told him we were going to ride there and that was that. I also used all of my dressage training and made sure I had his attention every single step of the way. Each time his eyes or head turned I jiggled my reins and got his attention back on me.

I had to do this about 200 times but it worked. After awhile (at the walk) he relaxed his neck, licked and chewed and began to give in to me. It's as if he said, "Okay leader you tell me where we're going."

It's all so basic and I already knew all of this it but needed you to remind me. It's also the way you described it that somehow it just clicked in my head.

What progress for us. Thanks again for your help with Jack it's meant so much already.

Lorna & Jack

Sometimes we need to look at ourselves to uncover the answers. Without even realizing it, we may be contributing to the problem. As you will read in Cecelia's story, everything we do can affect our animals' behavior.

Cecelia's High-Rise Dilemma

Sylvia contacted me when her little dog's behavior was causing her some pretty big problems. Living in a high-rise apartment in Oahu, Hawaii, Sylvia took Cecelia out frequently for exercise and trips to the dog park.

Apparently, Cecelia was growing more and more terrified of everything as each day went by. For her, each trip outside the safe haven of the apartment was a living nightmare of sounds,

Cecelia

people, other animals, traffic, you name it. Sylvia said that Cecelia would cower, shaking and trembling with fear.

When I connected with Cecelia, her energy was dim and what I saw as very fragile. She told me that she wasn't happy living this way, afraid of everything. Cecelia said she loved her mom, Sylvia, very much but didn't want to leave the apartment anymore.

Cecelia told me that she just didn't know what to do when faced with things that were scary to her. Sylvia had rescued Cecelia from a dire situation. It seemed that Cecelia's behavior was getting worse as time went by. As it was, Sylvia felt sorry for the little dog for having such a rough life before coming to live with her.

"I can't even have people over," Sylvia sighed as she explained her frustrations. "Cecelia gets so scared of visitors that she hides behind me or in the back room and won't come out."

I could understand how this made life difficult for Sylvia and Cecelia. When I asked Cecelia what her mom did when she acted scared, Cecelia showed me that mom picked her up and comforted her tiny, shaking body.

"Sylvia, tell me what you do when Cecelia displays this fearful behavior," I asked.

"Well, I usually pick her up and soothe her. I tell her everything is okay, and I won't let anything hurt her."

What Sylvia didn't realize was that picking up Cecelia was exactly the opposite of what she needed to do. Sylvia was actually perpetuating Cecelia's fearful behavior.

I explained to a surprised Sylvia that she needed to be firm but gentle with Cecelia. Whenever Cecelia displayed these fears, Sylvia needed to send her a firm but gentle message, either out loud or in her mind, to relax, sit and stay.

Once Sylvia got the hang of this new response, Cecelia's behavior changed dramatically.

I received this note from Sylvia:

Dear Karen,

Cecelia and I can't thank you enough for all of your help. I can take her anywhere now and she doesn't get nervous or scared anymore. I had no idea that I was part of her problem. You have changed both of our lives for the better.

Thank you so much,
Sylvia & Cecelia

Cecelia's case was easy to solve because Sue cared enough to listen to what Cecelia needed. Many times, we think we know the best way to handle a situation, but in reality it causes even more disruptive behavior.

Step outside of your situation and look at it from another perspective. Instead of blaming herself and feeling bad about her actions, Sue let go of the blame and made the right changes. Letting go of blame and guilt can be a difficult task for some. Those are two very big pills to swallow.

In the next chapter, you'll see how sometimes facing your biggest fears can move you forward into a happier, more balanced existence.

7

Illness
and Healing

Dakota

My husband's horse, Dakota, came down with some kind of digestive problem in March 2003. I'll never forget the panic I felt as I went out to the barn to feed the horses and saw Dakota on the ground, writhing in pain. As I ran to her side, I wondered how long she'd been down. From what I could determine, it looked pretty serious. I've had several horses with colic in the past, and I was all too familiar with the symptoms. I ran to the nearest phone and called the vet.

The tears were now stinging in my eyes as I stood there helpless, watching Dakota flail in pain. I threw myself on the ground next to her head and sobbed hysterically, "Please don't die, Dakota, please don't die. I'm not ready to lose you yet, please, please!"

I connected with Dakota's energy and immediately felt a blast of air like a snort in my face.

"You need to go away!" she demanded. "Just go away!"

Caught by surprise, I backed up. I hadn't realized that my hysterical behavior was upsetting her even more. All the panic that I was feeling was being sent right to Dakota.

"My belly hurts!" she cried. "It hurts! Just go away!"

I apologized to her and stepped back farther, waiting for the vet to arrive.

Dakota's critical condition sent her to the intensive care facility about twenty-five miles from our home. It was a pretty bleak outlook, and we were very worried.

After a complete exam and diagnostic tests, the only thing the doctors could tell me was that Dakota had some kind of bowel obstruction. They suggested an ultrasound to determine if it was a tumor or some other mass.

We obtained the ultrasound the next day, and the results did not bring good news. It was some kind of hard mass, about the size of a volleyball. Surgery was almost certainly the only way to remove it, but with Dakota almost eighteen years old and with a longstanding heart murmur, there was little chance of anyone agreeing to operate. This was heartbreaking news. Her condition continued to deteriorate.

When I visited Dakota, she stood limp in her stall, head hanging lifelessly, eyes barely open.

I sent her healing energy every day, as many times as I could. I pictured her in that stall, and I repeatedly told her to "just poop it out, Dakota. Lift your tail and just poop it out."

Dakota actually thought that was a pretty funny message, and she made a feeble attempt to laugh. I showed Dakota, in my mind, a rather grotesque picture of her spraying the inside of her pen with manure, all over the walls like a giant manure fountain.

"Okay, mom, I'll try," she said in a tiny whisper. She had been taken off food now for five days in an attempt to stop the mass from building. There were no other options for Dakota. Her heart murmur was too severe to proceed with surgery. The mass was hard and felt like it was calcified, according to the doctors.

My husband, Dan, and I continued to visit Dakota. Each time it looked worse, and we began to prepare for that ultimate, horrible decision. It just wasn't fair to let her stand there and suffer, to allow her to be in that much pain. We had to do something.

Dan and I agreed to visit her one last time and give our authorization for euthanasia. I prayed so hard that night, and I again told Dakota to just get rid of that impaction like she was painting the stall with manure. Her response was barely audible.

"I send you both my love," she responded, weak and very tired.

In a final attempt to get someone to operate, I made a few phone calls the next day to see if Washington State University veterinarians would at least examine her before saying "no." WSU has a fabulous veterinary program, and doctors there perform many types of advanced procedures with their state-ofthe-art equipment.

They agreed to an exam but gave me no hope other than that. I would have to take Dakota from the intensive care facility and trailer her down to the university. It was a long trip, not the best thing for an ailing horse.

I was on my way to pick her up when I got a call from my vet, Dr. Gary. He was a bit hesitant as he spoke, so I assumed he had more bad news for me.

"I don't know how to tell you this, Karen," he said rather awkwardly.

I pulled the truck over to the side of the road. I was sure this was going to be an unpleasant call.

"I went to check on Dakota, and when I looked inside her stall, there was manure everywhere. It was all over the walls. Then I examined her, and the obstruction was gone. I really don't know what to say except that none of us can feel any more obstruction. We don't see any point in keeping her here. She can go home."

I sat there on the side of the road with tears pouring down my face. A smile slowly began to turn up the corners of my mouth. I had told Dakota to spray the walls of her stall like a giant manure fountain, and she had done what I'd asked her to do. I couldn't believe it!

I pulled back onto the highway and headed toward the veterinary facility. Dakota came home and has been fine ever since. The massive ball turned out to have been a giant food obstruction that had hardened in her intestines. The combination of fluids she was receiving and Dakota's willingness to "paint the walls of her stall," led to a full recovery.

This experience taught me many things about stressful situations. When we express too much of any emotion, worry, panic, fear or doubt, those feelings go out like a tidal wave and hit our animals in their already weakened states. Stay calm if at all possible, think clearly for recovery, send powerful healing energy to your animals. Just remember, if it's their time to go, there is not much even a skilled surgical team can do.

It's never easy when our animals are in pain, but keeping your own emotions in check will make it an easier journey for them. Here's a simple prayer to invoke healing:

In a reverent manner, begin a silent, meditative prayer.

Calling upon the Universal Healing Energy, calling the angels of healing, come to (animal's name) now and surround him/her with healing.

Imagine the angels around the animal now, bringing love and warmth. Allow the brilliant White Light to cascade over his/her head and shoulders, back and chest, legs and belly, hips and legs, sending comfort and peace and healing energy to every cell in the body.

I ask for the highest and best outcome for (animal's name), and leave it in the hands of the Highest Power of the Universe. What is meant to be will be. Amen.

The power of prayer cannot be measured. It's a resource that I call upon for both humans and animals. Be respectful and always honor the outcome, whatever that may be.

Dakota healed from her ordeal. But in the next story, a healing of a different kind occurred.

Healing an Old Wound

Ellen came to see me in Los Angeles to connect with her deceased dog, Pal. Pal was a happy-go-lucky lab mix and was Ellen's constant companion during her junior high school years.

One day, while Ellen was inside a grocery store, someone took Pal from where she had him tied outside. Ellen was devastated. She couldn't control her tears even as she told me the story forty years later. All she could think about were the horrible things that must have happened to her beloved friend. She imagined all of the worst possible scenarios: That he had been stolen, then sold for animal experimentation, tortured or brutalized. All kinds of horrible things. Ellen couldn't get past the pain, and she blamed herself all those years for Pal's fate.

When I connected with Pal, he came through as the joyous, happy soul Ellen remembered. When I asked him what happened on that fateful day at the store, Pal showed me that another human had taken him away from the store. He described being surrounded by many other dogs, and it was very noisy and chaotic. He expressed his deep love for Ellen and how much he missed their daily escapades.

Afraid of what Pal might say, Ellen finally asked if he had been used for experiments.

"No, not at all. I was very loved," Pal answered, and with that he showed me a woman I would describe as being a hoarder of animals.

She loved and cared for her animals very much; she just had too many. Apparently, she felt that she could give Pal a better life than the person who had left him tied to a post, so she took him home. Pal lived out the rest of his life with her, very loved and very cared for. He told Ellen he would return to her one day so they could finish out their life with a happier ending.

This emotional session brought huge relief to Ellen, who sat motionless, tears pouring down, during the entire session. Overwhelmed with relief, she thanked me, hugged me and told me how much she appreciated hearing what had actually happened. A few weeks later, I received this letter:

Dear Karen,

Pal and I had been best friends since junior high. Then I made some poor choices and we found ourselves living in an unfortunate situation a thousand miles from home. We depended on one another for everything in life that was good. Then just like that he was stolen, and we never saw one another again.

For 40 years I have grieved for Pal and have harbored a deep sense of guilt over losing him. Worst of all has been living with my imagination over what his fate may have been.

After you made contact with Pal, I have finally been able to set him free. But every once in a while I almost feel him there

*next to me. It is wonderful Karen, thank you so much from Pal
as well as me for all you have done.*

Love,
Ellen K.

Holding on to years of grief or guilt is something I did myself. Harboring negative thoughts brings even more anguish to our souls. Forgiving ourselves is the first step toward closure and peace. It doesn't mean we have to forget what happened, but we can look into our hearts and see that we never intended to cause any harm.

Animals are very forgiving and want us to remember them in positive, loving ways. They love it when we say their names or think about them with smiles on our faces.

In the next chapter, you'll get a glimpse of animals' sometimes profound understanding of humans.

8

Lost Animals

Shadow

Shadow – Letting Go

Dealing with lost animals is almost always tough. It can be frustrating for the client, for me and for the animal. Normal communication sessions are done with animals that are safe and sound at home. The messages tend to be loving and free of trauma. But lost animals are in a panic. Their humans are frantic. These raw emotions alone can skew the messages. Because of the intense amount of time involved, and the extreme difficulty in general, I will only take lost-animal calls on a case-by-case basis.

It's like putting together a puzzle. It takes many sessions and countless hours of work on everyone's part to find a lost animal. So I try to follow my heart and help those who are truly prepared for the task, both physically and emotionally. Here are some of the lost-animal calls I decided to accept.

I was on my way to the home of some friends in October 2005, to feed their animals while they were on vacation. On a dirt road in Chattaroy, Washington, I saw a blue truck stopped in the middle of the road. I approached the truck and noticed a female driver, just sitting there, looking very distraught. I stopped and asked if everything was okay.

"No," she said painfully. "Have you seen a black dog running around here?"

"No, I haven't, but I'll keep my eyes open. What's your dog's name?"

"Shadow," the woman replied. "She took off about an hour ago, and I can't find her. She never does this."

I could sense this woman's distress. I reached into my pocket. "Here's my card. Call me if you need me."

The woman looked at my "Animal Communicator" card, then looked up at me.

"I'll keep my eyes open for Shadow," I repeated. "Which house is yours, in case I see her?"

"First driveway on the left," she pointed down the road. "Okay. Good luck," I said, and drove off.

It was a cold and dreary October day in Washington. It would be getting below freezing soon. I checked my friend's animals for her, made sure everyone was secure, and headed home. I didn't see the black dog anywhere.

Several days later, I received a call from Shadow's mom, Jen.

"Hi," she said on my voice mail. "I'm the one with the lost black dog, Shadow. She still isn't home, and I need your help."

I scheduled an appointment with Jen and, when the time came, I connected with Shadow right away.

"Is she still alive?" Jen asked, fearing the answer.

"Oh yes," I replied. "She's alive but she's hunkered down somewhere and very scared. She tells me she's very disoriented and that she's about five miles south of your house."

"Shadow was put on medication for seizure, and it was messing her head up." Jen stated with frustration in her voice. "I think that's why she took off." I soldiered on.

"Shadow is telling me that she's afraid to go to people she has seen, and she's showing me a wide-open field with a barbed wire fence."

This could have been anywhere in this area, and we both knew it.

"Shadow says she's hunkered down near an old, wrecked truck near this fence and this big field," I announced, trying to garner as many clues as I could from the frightened dog.

We finished that session, and Jen went searching for Shadow again. Her search took her door-to-door, among farms and pastureland. She posted signs everywhere in this farming region, and spoke to anyone she could about Shadow. Jen even found several other lost dogs while she was searching for Shadow, returning them to their homes.

Jen called me every day over the next week to have me check in on Shadow and to see if I could get any more clues from her. Sadly, there were no sightings, and no one called because of the signs. It was as if Shadow had vanished into thin air.

With Shadow still missing and her stress mounting, Jen's frustration continued to grow. I could connect with Shadow, get images of where she was and that she was alive, but she seemingly couldn't be found. It was a nightmare for Jen. In her desperation, she decided to contact another psychic to see if she could get more insight, or perhaps closure, on Shadow's disappearance.

After her session with this psychic, Jen called me in tears, telling me that Shadow was indeed dead. The other psychic had confirmed that the death process had started about three or four days before and that I was connecting with Shadow's spirit energy. She said she could see Shadow standing at Jen's side, in spirit form, looking up at her.

Jen thanked me for my efforts and told me she was going to say goodbye to Shadow with a quiet ceremony at home. Jen resigned herself to the fact that Shadow was dead. She was emotionally spent.

A few days later I was awakened at sunrise by a deep, resonating voice. It was Shadow's energy, but the voice was stronger and more powerful than I had remembered from our sessions. Shadow told me that her mom, Jen, needed to learn to let go. This was one of the lessons Shadow was trying to teach Jen. Once Jen let go, Shadow would return to her.

Shadow acknowledged that this lesson would be difficult and would create intense emotional trauma, but it was necessary for Jen's spiritual growth. Again Shadow showed me that she was still alive, just very cold (it was November now) and very hungry.

I felt compelled to deliver Shadow's messages to Jen even though she told me that she now believed Shadow was dead. When I called her, Jen told me how she'd had a quiet ceremony in Shadow's honor the night before, and said her final goodbyes. Jen listened quietly to the words Shadow had shared with me, thanked me again, and said she was now relieved to have closure.

Several days later, I received an ecstatic e-mail from Jen: "Shadow is alive and home!"

I got goose bumps as I read that! I called Jen immediately to hear what had happened. Jen said that several days after my sunrise messages from Shadow, and after her ceremony to say goodbye to Shadow, a man and his son called her to say they had seen one of her signs and had found Shadow in some tall grass, hunkered down in a ball near an airstrip for radio-controlled airplanes, in a large open field. The airstrip was roughly five miles south of Jen's home.

Shadow was so weak, shivering and so extremely thin she couldn't walk. The man and his son had to carry her back to the truck. It had been two weeks since she'd run off, but a veterinarian determined that Shadow was going to be okay.

It was a joyous reunion! After Shadow regained her strength, Jen brought her over to meet me in person. I was extremely moved by the connection between Shadow and Jen. It was a deep bond, deeper than I may ever understand.

As for the other psychic who said Shadow was dead: In my opinion, the Universe played out exactly the way it needed to. For without the other psychic telling her Shadow had died, Jen never would have fully "let go." Shadow gave me clear, accurate and detailed messages not only about where she was, but also about important lessons she was here to share with Jen.

After her return, Shadow's seizures disappeared for almost a year. Sadly, just before Jen was to leave for Iraq in January 2006, Shadow's seizures returned with a vengeance, and Jen truly had to say goodbye.

Shadow spent only ten years with Jen, but the lessons and memories she shared will last a lifetime.

Boo Boo

Anita contacted me one day about her missing, six year-old Shih Tzu/Yorkie mix, Boo Boo. It seems that on July 3, 2006, Anita was visiting her sister in Idaho. Anita left Boo Boo in the back yard, which had a chain-link fence around it.

Anita didn't think twice about the possibility of fireworks, as these were illegal in her own community at home. But here in Idaho, fireworks were allowed, and they went off throughout the night. Meanwhile, the sisters left to go see a movie. When they returned, Boo Boo was gone.

Apparently, terrified of the fireworks, he had managed to scale the chain-link fence. A frantic search of the neighborhood produced nothing. Anita said they had been looking for Boo Boo for about two days when she remembered seeing an article about me in the local newspaper.

This was Anita's first experience with an animal communicator, and she was desperate. To make matters worse, Anita's two small children were heartbroken over the loss of Boo Boo.

When I connected with Boo Boo, he showed me that he was on something soft, like carpet, and he sent me vivid images of ducks at a pond. He told me he was very scared and wanted to come home. He showed me that he was being restrained but, other than that, his messages were very confusing.

"Oh yes, I take Boo Boo to the pond, and he loves to bark at the ducks," Anita said in a sad voice. "I even checked that park again to see if he somehow made it there, trying to find his ducks."

I could hear her voice starting to crack with emotion.

As often happens with lost animals, the messages can be confusing and out of order, but Boo Boo couldn't even tell me for sure if he was still alive. I had to tell Anita that, at this point, I wasn't sure. We would have to see what other messages he sent.

At certain times during a session, the emotions from the animals and the humans can interfere with my connection, much like when you stand too close to a microwave on a cordless phone. The connection becomes raspy and broken.

"You are just going to have to wait for that phone call," I told her, "Someone will find him...."

Frustrated, Anita contacted another psychic for help. This one told her that raccoons had killed Boo Boo and that he was in the spirit world. Anita called me back for confirmation of her little dog's death.

I remained unconvinced that Boo Boo had died. Boo Boo's messages were confusing, but his energy was still in his physical body. When I connected with Boo Boo the second time, the messages were clear and descriptive.

Boo Boo showed me what looked like a public restroom at a campground. I told Anita to look for a statue of some kind and, from that point, she needed to "look up and see where Boo Boo was being held."

I described a panoramic view from this place, and said it was about a mile from her sister's house. I also saw the woman who had Boo Boo. She was in her mid to late forties, with shoulderlength, graying brown hair. She had some kind of disability and walked with a distinct limp. I felt her energy to be somewhat irrational and difficult to deal with.

I described this woman's house as being very average, square and non-descript. I couldn't make out a color, but it appeared very bland. It looked like some kind of farm or other agricultural facility, but not huge. I saw shiny roofs made of metal and a ridgeline of trees behind the house. I saw a camper or RV in the driveway, and it looked rather uncared for. There seemed to be a lot of activity around this house, and there was a lot of negative energy moving around.

Anita set out with this new information, trying to find her beloved dog. Shortly after this session, Boo Boo was indeed located. It appeared that he had left her sister's house and run to a rodeo ground area (which had seemed like a campground to me), complete with a public restroom, about a mile away. Anita went to this place and found a bucking bronco statue, as I had described. The woman who had Boo Boo lived near this statue, along a ridgeline of trees. Anita said that if you went to this statue and looked up, you could see the woman's home.

The woman lived in a beige, ranch style house with her husband, who had just baled the hay in their fields. There was a motor home in the driveway, and the outbuildings had shiny metal roofs. They had teenaged children, and the police suspected drug activity there. The woman was very irrational and argumentative. She indeed was in her mid to late forties and had graying brown, shoulder-length hair.

A pet groomer from a local store called Anita, having recognized Boo Boo from a flyer that Anita mailed to the shop. The groomer said that a woman had come in with a dog that looked just like Boo Boo, but they didn't have any slots open at that time, so she scheduled a time for later that week. The groomer collected the woman's information and promptly called Anita.

Anita went to the local police to report the incident. The first few times the police went out to the address, the people said they didn't have a dog. Then they said the woman who had the dog had moved away. Police saw through all this and decided to show up unannounced one day. Lo and behold, there was Boo Boo on the front porch!

Without Anita's determination, Boo Boo might never have made it back into her arms. Both are together again, and Anita never lets him out of her sight. When Boo Boo was returned to Anita, he still had on his old collar, had a bad ear infection, but was otherwise in good health.

Boo Boo's ordeal had lasted three and a half weeks.

Finding a lost animal takes great effort by everyone concerned. Anita was relentless, and continued to follow her own feelings to keep up the search.

Sassy: Lost in Oklahoma

Jeannie called me frantically one day when her beloved Lhasa Apso mix, Sassy, ran away during a fierce storm. Sassy was terrified of thunder, and Jeannie called a neighbor from work and asked her to get Sassy out of the back yard until Jeannie got home that night. Unfortunately, when the neighbor opened the gate, the terrified dog ran down the street and disappeared into the rain.

After a frantic search for help, Jeannie found me on the Internet. She wanted to set up an appointment right away, as is the case with owners of most lost animals. Time was critical, and Jeannie had already searched for over a week with no luck.

Jeannie lived alone, and Sassy was her life. She took Sassy everywhere with her: shopping, errands, visiting family and friends. The two were inseparable. Jeannie was sick with grief and guilt the first time we spoke. She thought for sure that her beloved Sassy was dead somewhere, and Jeannie believed it was all her fault.

I calmed her down and explained how important it is to keep our emotions calm during a session. As hard as it was for her to focus, Jeannie realized this could be her link to Sassy, and she managed to calm herself.

Sassy was an adorable little dog with long, fluffy fur and the sweetest face. I connected with her instantly, and got a very excited response. I told Sassy that her mom, Jeannie, was with me, and we were trying to find her. I explained to the little dog how important it would be to send me clear images of where she was and what she was experiencing.

I received several messages from Sassy that she was still alive. I often ask animals to tell me what they feel beneath their feet. If they describe something as hard, cold, damp, dark, rough, grass-like, etc., then chances are they are still alive. When they say they can't feel anything, or it's just all soft around them, or if I get a floating sensation, chances are they have passed into the spirit world.

There are exceptions to this, of course, and I'll cover one in the next story.

Sassy told me that she was warm and had a full tummy. She said she was terribly confused and wanted to come home. Where was her mom? She wanted to know. I assured her that mom was trying very hard to find her. Sassy also sent me images of being inside of a house, and I saw floral patterns on the couch and lacy, frilly window coverings.

With this new information, Jeannie was relentless in her search. She posted flyers, offered rewards, and placed ads in local newspapers for any information on Sassy's whereabouts. A few people called, but none of the dogs turned out to be Sassy.

During one of Jeannie's sessions, I called upon higher sources, my spirit guides and angels, to help me with Sassy's location. Many times the animals don't know where they are, so I call upon this guidance. Guidance came through very clearly that Sassy was north of her home, and I saw the number ten. Guidance was telling me that she was about ten miles or ten minutes from home. I was able to determine that it was ten miles.

I also saw the woman who had Sassy. This was an eccentric person, one who would raise an eyebrow with most folks. I saw that she took Sassy with her in the car when she left each day to do errands. She was taking good care of Sassy, but she had no intention of finding her rightful home. I also received a very clear image of this woman's vehicle, which had a military reference on the bumper, like some kind of sticker or saying. The woman was retired. I saw gray hair, and she wore glasses. She was on the heavy side.

Focusing on Sassy's messages, I was also able to get an image of a male energy living with this woman. This wasn't her husband, I told Jeannie. The woman wasn't married, but this male energy was somehow connected with her. That male energy was more agreeable than the woman's energy. He was actually trying to persuade the woman to return Sassy to her proper owner.   From what I saw, the woman wouldn't cooperate. These images came to me like mini movies playing in my head; little bits and pieces that I put together.

Jeannie asked if I could get a description of the house, or the street name. This can be very difficult, but I told her I'd try. I saw a white or light-colored, older house, with a front step or porch. It seemed a bit tattered. I suggested that Jeannie look for a Berry Street or Mulberry Street.

The yard looked untidy and not very manicured. I also saw a religious statue out front and a pile of bricks or concrete near the sidewalk. Jeannie wrote down all the clues I got, then she was off again in her quest for Sassy.

Even with ads in every paper and on the radio, and with flyers posted all over the city, no one came forward with any information on Sassy. Frustrated with the whole experience, Jeannie was at her wits' end. She wanted to continue her search, but without some kind of lead it was like looking for the proverbial needle in a haystack. She had driven up and down every street in that ten-mile radius, looking for the house or car I had described to her. Her patience and her nerves were wearing down.

I tell my clients that I'll support them no matter what they decide. If they feel they can't continue the search, I'll back them on that. If they want me to keep checking in with their lost animals, I'll do so. It's a personal decision. Every person is different; every situation is different.

Several weeks later, about six weeks after Sassy's disappearance in that rainstorm, Jeannie got the break she was hoping and praying for. A woman who'd seen one of the flyers called to say that her mother in-law had recently found a dog that matched Sassy's picture. The only problem was that she was not willing to give the dog back.

The woman explained that her mother in-law was a little bit "different" and wouldn't listen to reason. Jeannie pleaded with this woman to give her the location of the dog, just so she could rule it out if it wasn't Sassy.

The woman finally agreed to give her the address, saying that her brother-in-law, this "different" woman's son, lived there too. She noted that he might be able to convince the woman to give up the dog if it was indeed Sassy.

The address she gave Jeannie was on Mulberry Street.

Jeannie called me in a panic as she ran out the door, promising to let me know as soon as she was sure. Jeannie headed toward Mulberry Street with tears in her eyes. Could this be the eccentric woman I had described to her? Could the brother-in-law be the male energy connected with her?

Almost an hour went by before I heard from Jeannie again. It was indeed Sassy! She was okay, and she was home again, safe and sound.

Jeannie was elated, and said that everything I'd told her had checked out. The woman was retired, on the heavy side, and lived with her son. He had been giving his mom a hard time because she wanted to keep the dog. She had found Sassy that stormy day, wet, shivering and cold on a busy street corner just around the block from Jeannie's home. Angry that anyone would let such a lovely little dog loose in such a storm, the woman decided to keep the dog as her own.

She and her son lived in a house that was a bit tattered, with lacy curtains in the front window that framed the floral-patterned sofa. It was just over ten miles from Jeannie's front door. There was no front porch, but there was a large stoop.

The woman also drove a metallic-gold, four-door sedan with a yellow ribbon "Save our Troops" bumper sticker. There was a statue of the Virgin Mary in her front yard, and the city was repaving the street, so there were big chunks of asphalt and road base on the side of the road.

Not all lost-animal stories have happy endings. In the next story, about Mollie, a dog's perilous attempt to cross a dangerous river ended in tragedy.

Mollie's story

Sometimes when animals die suddenly or unexpectedly, they just don't realize they are no longer on this Earth. It's similar to what happens in the 1990 film *Ghost*, with Patrick Swayze and Demi Moore. The character, Sam, dies suddenly and can't figure out why no one can see or hear him. Sam hasn't realized that he has died. Humans and animals experience something very similar to this. They continue to send messages as though they're still alive and well, hungry, tired or scared.

In reality, they've crossed over into the spirit world and are just not ready to accept their fates. Fortunately, this doesn't last long, as a guardian spirit or deceased family member will often appear and help them transition. There can be a sort of inbetween space, between Earth and the other side. I've also heard it described as a gray/blue area or the hazy area.

This is one reason why lost-animal calls are so difficult. Even though the animal sends messages that he or she is alive and well, there's the chance that there's just no realization of having crossed over. It's my job to deliver the message exactly as I get it from the animal, as was the case with Mollie.

Mollie was a gorgeous, black lab mix, loyal and devoted to her human, Matt. Matt lived in Colorado and often took Mollie with him on his hiking adventures into the back woods and beautiful Colorado Mountains. When Matt and some friends decided to go to an area that had a river with rapids, Mollie came along as usual.

During the hike, Mollie and Matt became separated. Matt searched relentlessly for her long into the dark hours of the night. Devastated, Matt called his parents, who also lived in Colorado. He told them Mollie was gone and that he was staying to search for her. In desperation, Matt's parents called me, hoping that I could reunite their son and his dog.

I connected with Mollie and immediately felt her intense love for Matt. She showed me countless hikes and trips they had taken, and all the fun they had had together. Mollie told me she was okay but was very upset about being separated from Matt. I told her I would do my best to help them find each other in this vast wilderness.

The Four Corners area, where Mollie was lost, has hundreds of trails that zigzag through the mountains. Trying to find something in her messages that would stand out, such as a landmark, was very difficult. Mollie sent many messages to me about her love for Matt. She had the best life, she told me, with a big smile on her face.

Finally, Mollie showed me that she was on or near a large rock outcropping. I could see where the tree line ended and exposed rock began. Here at last was something I could give to Matt's parents. I described the area as best I could. Mollie also showed me a river that looked pretty deep and fast. She told me she was scared and just wanted to go home. I assured her that Matt was out looking for her every day, and that he wouldn't stop until he found her.

I got a sad phone call several days later. A hiker had found Mollie's body washed up along the shoreline, and remembered the flyers he had seen about the lost black lab. As far as could be told, Mollie had been dead for several days. Apparently, Mollie had tried to follow Matt across the river and had perished in the fast-moving water. We were all devastated.

Mollie had sent so many messages that she was okay and scared, and had showed me the rock outcropping where she was waiting for Matt. Mollie was still earthbound, not realizing she had passed. I called her angels to her to help her transition to the other side.

Finding a lost dog can be difficult, but most dogs stay "visible" and can travel great distances in search of home.

Cats can be particularly difficult to find. Even an outgoing, friendly cat can become skittish and fearful when lost in unfamiliar territory. Cats are normally very homebound and have a connection to the Earth that dogs don't seem to have. They usually know their neighborhoods and travel the same paths to their hunting grounds or other favorite spots. In one case, a cat decided to go back to his old hunting grounds.

Finding Mo

From a small farming town in Virginia comes the story of Mo. Mo's mom, Tara, called me shortly after Mo's disappearance from their rural home. Usually, Mo didn't travel farther than the barn, his mom explained to me, but when he hadn't come home for dinner a few nights before, Tara knew something was wrong.

Mo was a black cat with no other markings. Just black. I immediately connected with Mo, and he showed me what looked like a large area covered with snow. I told Tara what I was seeing, and she laughed, explaining they live among cotton fields. They had just harvested the cotton, so the fields were covered in white!

Mo was definitely on the move; it was just a matter of where. Mo continued to show me images of cows, barns, tractors, silos, old trucks, farmers and their overalls. Tara would call me from various locations in her area so we could see if this matched what Mo was seeing.

Weeks passed without a sign of Mo. Whenever I checked in with him, he sent me messages that he was alive, fine and a little "plump," so he was having no trouble finding food.

Cats become very resourceful when lost. They revert to survival mode, and the instincts kick in. This can be good and bad. Good because they can find food, water and shelter but bad because the often become skittish and won't even come if their human calls them.

Mo

Cats will often travel only at dawn and dusk, finding a safe spot to stay during the day. They usually don't go far from home, either. Most cats are found only a few blocks away, or within a mile or less of home. They do like to hide in the tiniest crawlspaces imaginable.

Finding a lost cat is, once again, like finding that infamous needle in a haystack!

Mo gave me images of being on the move. He wasn't hunkered down. He would show me outbuildings, farmhouses and piles of bricks. Mo wasn't the typical lost cat. It was like Mo was on a mission.

After nine long weeks and countless dead ends and black-cat sightings, Tara's nerves were frayed and her frustration was wearing her down. With no collar or other markings, it's almost impossible to identify black cats from a distance. Most would scurry off before Tara even got close.

Tara had me check in with Mo one more time. This time, he showed me white houses with green trim. I saw a triangular type of setting, like a park or ball field. I also saw very manicured grass. Mo also showed me "pink things" in the grass.

These clues were certainly very different from what he had sent us before. I was able to call upon spiritual guidance to see about how far from home Mo was. I saw a fifteen, as in fifteen miles. This was much farther away than Tara had been looking.

She was ready to give up when the phone suddenly rang. It was the woman calling from Tara's former home. She said, "Hey, are you missing Mo? He just walked into the barn and started eating the cat's food like he owned the place!"

"Yes, I'm missing Mo!" Tara yelled. "Is it really him?"

"I think so," she replied. "He's kind of chubby."

Tara drove as fast as she could the fifteen miles to her old house and barn. If Mo had gone in a straight line back to his old barn it was probably only about eight miles away. But Mo took the scenic route: zigzagging across the fields and pastures.

As she drove up to the house, Tara passed a ball field not far from the barn, with a triangular shape and a manicured lawn.

Once she was in the driveway, Tara saw that the house had been painted white with green trim, and the new tenants had pink and brightly colored children's toys lying around the yard! Mo had sent all of these images to me! Tara was truly amazed! She ran to the barn, picked up her chubby black cat and gave him the biggest hug she could!

Mo now wears a lime-green collar and is only allowed outside when Tara is home to supervise. All black cats look the same!

9

Mirrors

Bailey

In the numerous sessions I've done, it has become apparent that our animals are like our own personal barometers. They often reflect the state of our own minds, our lives, and the calm or turmoil within. Animals are also our healers, and many times they are here to help us overcome illness or injury or to assist us through difficult times.

At an expo in Spokane, Washington, I sat down with Dana, who wanted a session with her Pug, Bella. Bella was about three years old and very much the apple of her mom's eye. Dana wanted me to check on Bella, whom she said had been "acting strange" lately.

When I connected with Bella, the first thing she said was, "I don't want to go, I don't want to go."

Bella was very insistent, but wouldn't tell me anything more. So I said to Dana, "Bella is telling me that she doesn't want to go somewhere. Do you know what she's talking about?"

Suddenly, Dana burst into tears. Happy and smiling one minute, crying and sobbing the next, I had no idea what I'd said to upset her.

"Dana, are you okay?" I asked. I wasn't sure if I should go forward with the session.

"I'm s-sorry," she stammered. "I'm so sorry! Look at me, crying like a baby. It's me. It's me she's talking about. I'm the one who doesn't want to go."

Dana was finally able to tell me that her husband had just been transferred to Kentucky, and they were going to have to pack up their entire lives and move across the country. Apparently, Dana's grown children, and soon to be grandchildren, all lived in Spokane, and Dana didn't want to leave her hometown.

Bella, Dana's little barometer, had picked up on her feelings of not wanting to go. Although Bella couldn't tell me any more, she knew her mom was upset about it, so it upset her too. As a result, Bella didn't want to go either. That's why she'd been acting strangely.

Our animals pick up on our human emotions, but they're not always able to understand the reasons behind our stress.

Animals remind us to keep our lives balanced, taking time for ourselves and doing the things we truly enjoy.

Bailey's mysterious illness

Darleen contacted me for a session with her rescued border collie mix, Bailey. Bailey was exhibiting some odd behavior, including an unusual lack of energy.

"I don't know what's wrong with him," Darleen said. "He used to go over and play with his friend, Max, and now he just lies around moping all day long."

Darleen had taken Bailey to the vet to rule out an infection or some other health issue, and after hundreds of dollars in blood tests, the vet could find nothing wrong with him.

"All his test results are normal," Darleen sighed. "It's like he's lost his zest for life, and he's only three years old."

I checked in with Bailey to see what he had to say. I always give the animals a chance to tell me what's on their minds or what messages they have for their moms or dads first. Many times, it can be more important than the questions we ourselves have for them.

Bailey's energy came through as very dull, very low. Border collies are known for their high energy and never-ending stamina. Bailey's energy centers seemed blocked.

"I don't feel right," Bailey said. "I just don't feel like doing anything. I feel depleted."

With Bailey's permission, I entered his energy field so I could scan it and see what was going on. Looking into an animal's energy can tell me many different things. I can see areas of pain or discomfort, tumors or masses, bacteria or infection, arthritis, and many other ailments. To me, it looks very much like a living x-ray, an x-ray with colors and movement.

Bailey's energy centers, his chakras, were all full of what came across as debris and negative black spots. Normally, chakras are vibrant and spinning beautifully, but Bailey's were dark and dull. Humans and animals have these chakras, and they can become clogged with emotional and physical garbage. Cleaning them out, clearing them, can help bring back energy, zest and emotional balance.

As I was viewing Bailey's energy centers, I saw a mirroring effect between him and his mom, Darleen. As I looked at both of their energy fields, I saw an exact mirror of Bailey's dull, lifeless energy reflected in Darleen's energy field.

"Darleen, are you feeling okay," I asked carefully, not wanting to upset her.

"Yeah, I'm okay. Why do you ask?"

I told her what I saw in the energy fields, and that they were reflecting one another.

"Oh, my gosh!" she suddenly gasped. "I can't believe that! I would never have thought that until you said it!"

"Thought what?" I asked

"I have fibromyalgia. It's pretty bad sometimes."

I hadn't heard of this condition, so Darleen described it. Fibromyalgia syndrome affects the muscle fiber and connective tissues as a result of poor diet, lack of exercise, stress, physical and/or emotional trauma, and toxicity from air, water, refined foods, and our own metabolisms. The result is widespread pain and exhaustion. The sufferer loses the ability to reach deep sleep, the energy cycle shuts down, and the immune system becomes severely compromised. Strengthening the immune system is the key to healing.

Darleen's painful and debilitating condition was being mirrored in Bailey's energy field. This session helped Darleen realize that she needed to do more to keep herself healthy and that by doing so, Bailey would stay healthy as well.

The animals are here for us as our friends and companions, but they are also here to help us through illness or injury. Their unconditional love knows no bounds. As you will read in the next chapter, even animals who have crossed over to the spirit world stay connected with us, guiding us and assisting us from the other side.

10
Animals in the Afterlife

Tabby and Lisa

Tabby

L isa contacted me after hearing my interview on a local radio station in Spokane, Washington. An avid animal lover, Lisa had several animals at home she wanted to connect with. She finally decided to have me contact her deceased cat, Tabby.

Lisa had agonized over Tabby's death, and she felt terribly guilty about the circumstances surrounding it. Lisa hoped to make a connection with Tabby to tell her how very sorry she was and to tell the cat how much she missed her.

I contacted Tabby, and immediately her energy came through. Tabby said to tell her mom, Lisa, that she was not "gone."

"I'm here," Tabby said. "Right here by her side. I have never left. She mourns for me and grieves for me for no reason. There is no sadness in what happened. It was the Will of the Universe, and it was my time. I had other things to do and to accomplish, and she must realize this. Tell her for me, will you?"

"I will tell her Tabby. What other messages can you share?"

"Tell her I am fine and that this is a beautiful place. No one can imagine the beauty it fills. We are here for now, but in time we will move on and continue our journey. Our journey continues."

"Tabby, that sounds wonderful. Tell me what was your purpose for being with your mom, Lisa?"

"I filled her heart with joy and I gave her the confidence she needed. She is still fighting with this confidence, and I feel her struggle. Tell her she has it in her, she just needs to look. Perhaps hearing from me will encourage her to find her inner strength, the glory that lies within. Perhaps now she will start on her way, on the path to finding that strength."

"Perhaps she will, Tabby. I will tell her, but do you know that your mom still agonizes over your death, and that she blames herself? How do you feel about that?"

"There is no reason to blame oneself. This is the work of higher energies that determine what will be. She needs to realize that love never ends. It conquers all, and with this love in her heart she can conquer all. She is being tested right now, and part of her test came from me. But now she is still learning about her limits and her strengths, and she needs to know she has power beyond what she thinks. She just needs to pay attention to it."

"Then you don't hold her responsible for your passing?"

"No, my child, there is no one man or woman on this Earth who can be responsible for what the Elders decide. There are great energies at work beyond our consciousness. We do not determine things like life or death. She needs to know that she is not responsible for my time on Earth. My time on Earth is written as the Will and will be what it is. No one can alter that.

"Please tell her to release those feelings of blame and guilt, and to rejoice in the lessons of love that she learned. She opened her heart to me as she has to opened her heart to others. That was what needed to happen and it did, it happened. Great things will come to her. Tell her to focus and pay attention and great things will come."

"I will tell her, Tabby. What other message do you have for Lisa?"

"Tell her I am wise beyond (my years), and I have been in Spirit now and will continue to learn far faster than on Earth. Our time here in Spirit is no comparison to your time there. You cannot comprehend our time."

"Do you feel good?" I asked.

"I feel fine, I feel good! I have no pain, no worry, no regrets. I am complete. My energy completes itself here. We are all rejuvenated while we are here. It is our filling stop. We stop here and rest, and we are filled up with knowledge to continue our journeys."

"So you are not alone?"

"No, not at all. There are many of us here, all at our own pace. There is not a time frame. We do not have to come or go at any certain time, just when we are ready and feel fulfilled, then we continue on."

"Then what happens?"

"We go to our next place (assignment)."

"You mean back to this Earth?"

"Yes, if that is the Will."

"The Will of the Universe?"

"Yes, if that is the Will, then we come back and we continue to learn and to grow. We all grow on Earth and learn lessons, then we come here to be refreshed. It is quite nice here."

"Please tell me more about it."

"It is glorious, it is magnificent, it is all encompassing, and it is LOVE!"

"So you feel loved?"

"We all feel loved. This is our Creator, and we are all loved."

"So will your journey take you back to Lisa?"

"Perhaps. I feel she has more to learn."

"And you think you can teach her?"

"I already taught her much! Her lessons were valuable, and she completed them well."

"What did you teach her?"

"Compassion and trust."

"Those are wonderful lessons. I'm sure she appreciates that."

"Yes, but she wastes it on blame. Tell her not to waste. It is not necessary to waste such lessons on things like blame and guilt. These are not valued traits. They are worthless and take away from our value. Tell her to pay attention to the good, what she learned in her heart, to know that I am with her every day. I feel her pain and can do nothing but wait."

"Wait for what?"

"For her to realize that I am fine and she is fine too. Once she realizes this, it will all be…"

"Will all be what?"

"Complete."

"Oh, I see. So you'd like your mom, Lisa, to focus on the good, the lessons and the things she learned from you…"

"Yes, I opened her heart to these difficult things, and now she must continue her path."

"I see. Well, thank you Tabby. You have really helped me and your mom understand things a little better. I hope you realize how much she loves you."

"Oh, I do, my dear. There is love like no other."

"She continues to send her love to you."

"And I to her."

"Go in peace, my friend Tabby, until we meet again." "You as well, my dear. Goodbye!" Lisa's reply came to me via email.

Dear Karen:

Since hearing Tabby's thoughts and wisdom, I have filled a spot in my heart with joy that was sad for so long. I feel that this experience helped me realize the joy in my life and that blame and guilt are qualities that should not be stressed about for long.

In your conversation with Tabby, she said, "I filled her heart with joy and I gave her the confidence she needed. She is still fighting with this confidence and I feel her struggle. tTell her she has it in her, she just needs to look. Perhaps hearing from me will encourage her to find her inner strength, the glory that lies within. Perhaps now she will start on her way on the path to finding that strength."

By releasing blame and guilt in my life, my confidence has grown more than I could ever guess. Tabby's words are helping me beyond what I ever imagined is possible. I hope that I am making her proud and passing the test that I believe she gives me.

Thank you again, Karen, for this experience. Lisa

Baron

When Dave heard that I was an animal communicator, he asked for a session with his seven year-old German shepherd, Baron. Dave had a very close bond with Baron, but the dog's health had taken a turn for the worse. Dave was concerned that Baron was not eating properly and was just not himself.

Without knowing any more, I contacted Baron. Baron told me about the close connection he had with Dave, his human dad, and how fun his life was in the mountains, running through the woods and playing in the streams with Dave and his other dog. Baron showed me his favorite place in the house; a big sunlit room filled with floor-to-ceiling windows and plants.

When I asked Baron how he felt, his energy shifted. He told me he didn't feel that good and that his "heart hurt." I asked Baron if the pain in his heart was emotional or physical. Baron replied that it was actual pain.

He had no idea why his appetite was failing, but told me that he felt it was his "time to go." Baron sent his love to his dad and asked me to tell him how very special Dave made him feel.

I gave the messages to Dave, and, naturally, he was very upset. When I mentioned that Baron's heart hurt, Dave was amazed. Only he and his vet knew that Baron suffered from a heart condition. He hadn't shared this information with anyone.

As Dave listened to the messages from Baron, he grew very quiet. This man couldn't imagine life without Baron. They were constant companions and best friends.

Dave confirmed that his mountain home had a large entryway, with floor to ceiling windows, that was full of his wife's plants. I had never been to their home. Dave said that Baron loved to lie in that room so he could see everything that was going on outside. He also told me how he would take Baron and Reka, his other dog, on long walks through the Rocky Mountains, and the dogs would splash and play in the stream.

The vet continued to run tests on Baron to find out what was going on with his failing health.

About a week later, I was notified that Baron had passed into the spirit world. Dave had buried him on a hill overlooking the banks of the stream where he and Reka played. Dave thanked me for the messages from Baron, and said they brought him great comfort.

Two weeks later, I was quietly meditating at home when Baron's energy unexpectedly appeared to me. Baron told me he had an urgent message for Dave and that he needed to talk to me right away. Baron told me that he was very concerned that

Dave was still agonizing over his death. He knew that his dad was full of sorrow, sadness and loss.

Baron said this made him very upset, and requested that I contact Dave right away to say that Baron was still there, by his side. Baron said he would "never leave him" and that if Dave listened closely, he would hear Baron's collar jingling. Baron said that it was "his time to go and nothing could have changed that."

He wanted his dad to stop feeling guilty about his death. Instead, Baron asked that Dave remember him and all the wonderful times they had had, the great life they had shared, and the bonds of friendship that would never end.

Baron spoke with an urgency I couldn't ignore, so I made a very hesitant phone call to Dave. I hadn't spoken with him since Baron's passing, and I wasn't sure how he would take this unexpected call. Dave answered, and I told him to just listen, not to say one word. I delivered the urgent messages from Baron, then quietly hung up the phone before Dave could reply.

Several days later, Dave called me back. He told me that it was true; he had been agonizing over Baron's loss, full of sadness, and dwelling on guilt over Baron's death. He was blaming himself for not being able to find out what was wrong with Baron before he died. Dave said that at first he was a little stunned by Baron's messages from the spirit world. But once he thought about it, he realized that Baron was still with him.

Dave shifted his thoughts to all the wonderful times he and Baron had experienced together and the closeness they had shared. He said he had even felt Baron's presence several times, and he would listen for the sound of his collar jingling. Dave said that only Baron would have such a direct connection to his heart to know all those things about him and how badly he was struggling with the loss.

Now Dave knows that the bonds of love are eternal. They do not end with death. They continue forever.

It has been several years now since Baron passed into the spirit world. Dave still misses him and their daily walks, but now he and Reka take Kit, his new rescued German shepherd, through the mountains to play in the streams. And Dave knows in his heart that Baron is right there by his side every step of the way.

Kalea

Kalea's mom, Arti, called me soon after Kalea's passing. The seven year-old Schnauzer had died suddenly, leaving Arti devastated and unable to cope with her loss.

Arti was somewhat skeptical of the process, but after a friend recommended me, she finally agreed to call. Like many people, Arti wanted to know if there would be any specific messages from Kalea so she would know it was really her beloved dog coming through. I assured Arti that I would be able to connect with Kalea's energy, bringing many aspects about her personality and behaviors to the session. I also reminded her that I have no control over what animals tell me. I can ask questions, but only they control their answers.

This tearful phone session started on a sunny morning. I was in my office in Elk, Washington, and Arti was in Colorado. Immediately, Kalea sent Arti many loving messages and told her how sorry she was to see her mom in so much pain. Kalea reassured her mom that she was okay and adjusting to her new life in the spirit world. There were many heartfelt messages that came through, bringing much needed relief and tears of joy. As we neared the end of the session, Arti asked Kalea what her favorite memory was of their life together.

Kalea responded to me, "Tell her water in the grass, water in the grass."
Not knowing what this reference meant, I almost didn't say it.

"Tell her," Kalea nudged at me gently with her energy. "Tell her water in the grass."

Okay, I thought to myself, I've learned to just say whatever message comes through, no matter how strange it sounds to me.

"I'm supposed to tell that you her favorite memory is water in the grass."

There was silence on the other end of the phone, followed by a sharp intake of breath. "Oh, my dear!" Arti gasped, then softly started to cry.

"Tell me, Arti, what does this mean? What is water in the grass?"

Arti told me through her tears that her back yard had several levels. On one level she had a park bench next to a water fountain. One of her favorite things to do with Kalea was to go out back, sit on this bench and, as the water splashed out of the fountain onto the lawn, Kalea would bite at the water in the grass. It was a simple pleasure that they both enjoyed, and Kalea knew it was the message her mom needed to hear.

Arti was so touched, she was speechless. Even from the spirit world, Kalea relayed specific memories of their life together in such a simple way. Water in the grass. Sometimes it's the little things that mean the most to our animal companions.

Seeing Spots

Denice and her mom, Margaret, came to the Spokane Expo in June 2006 to check in on several of their animal companions, both living and deceased. Denice asked if I would connect with Sophie, who had recently passed.

Both Denice and Margaret were listening intently to Sophie's messages as I connected with the pretty gray-and-white kitty. Denice explained that she wanted to make sure that Sophie had made it to the other side so she could come back to her again in this or another lifetime.

Denice said she had agonized over the decision to euthanize Sophie some five weeks earlier, at about the same time that Margaret's dog, Blanch had passed. Denice still held a lot of guilt and grief over Sophie's passing. What she didn't realize was that her emotional ties to Sophie were keeping the cat Earthbound and unable to continue her journey to the Light.

As I connected with Sophie, I saw her claws firmly planted in the Earth, not wanting to let go. Sophie needed my help. Confused and not sure of what to do, I showed Sophie how there were angels there to help her cross over to the other side so she could continue her journey.

I'll explain how to do this in the next section.

With some simple visualizations, Sophie slowly started to release her grip.

Denice admitted that she was to blame for holding onto Sophie emotionally. She said she was being selfish and realized it was not helping Sophie's journey.

As I began to send Sophie toward her Angels, Sophie sent me a clear message that she was seeing spots.

"Why would she tell me that she's seeing spots?" I asked Denice, not sure what this message meant.

"I don't know," Denice shrugged, trying to understand what the "spots" could be.

Sophie was still reluctant to leave the Earth-plane, so I had to call upon her angels as if they were the cavalry, horns blaring, coming over a rise. It was quite a fabulous and divine scene. The angels came and surrounded Sophie with love, and let her know it was safe. Sophie still felt she couldn't let go.

"She still doesn't want to let go," I said to Denice and Margaret.

Margaret asked me if Sophie could see Blanch. If she could, that meant Sophie was able to make it to the spirit world. I asked Barbara to describe Blanch to me so I could picture her in my mind. Barbara just handed me Blanch's picture.

When I looked at the picture, I couldn't believe what I saw. Blanch was a border collie mix with huge black and white spots!

Sophie told me very clearly she was seeing "spots," seeing Blanch! Sophie was letting me know she was now able to let go and make it to the other side with Blanch!

"She's seeing spots!" I said. "Blanch is spotted! She has big cow spots!"

Denice and Margaret "got it" now too; the spot reference was to Blanch!

Sophie was so happy we all finally got the message that she started to make me laugh and smile.

It was a funny way of putting it together, but we all finally got it!

Timmy

When I first met Timmy, he stole my heart. He had that affect on people. This beautiful little black-and-white kitten had the face of an angel and a heart of gold.

He suffered from numerous afflictions, including *spina bifida*, or a curvature of the spine, and *cerebella hyperplasia*, which causes jerky movements or tremors.

Spina bifida*: The vertebrae fail to close normally around the spinal cord, leading to motor and sensory problems in areas fed by affected nerves. The Manx, in particular, suffers from this problem because it is associated with the gene for taillessness. Symptoms can also include a hopping gait and incontinence. Source: www.petsmart.com*

Timmy's mom, Jamie, is a special needs expert and also cares for Ricki Tik as discussed in an earlier chapter. Although Timmy

Timmy

had many physical challenges, the love poured from him, and he had many friends. He would lie on his towel with his kitty friends, or play with toys and even watch cat movies on the big screen.

Timmy especially liked the "movie with dogs," he told me one day. Jamie laughed as she remembered that another cat must have stepped on the remote and changed the channel to a dog show. Timmy loved to watch dogs on the big screen.

Jamie also took Timmy to his regular *cranial sacral* therapy sessions to help stimulate nerves and improve his overall health. When I checked in with Timmy, he said he loved his therapy sessions and he especially loved to go places with his mom.

Timmy fit nicely into a special sling that Jamie made for him, and he traveled with her as she ran errands or spent time outside in the sunshine. He was truly the joy of her life. He never complained, even with all the physical challenges he faced. He shared only his love and devotion to his mom and his favorite toys.

On a late winter evening, I got a call from Jamie. Timmy had passed away suddenly, unexpectedly, and she was devastated.

There had been little that Jamie or anyone else could do. Rushed to the emergency vet clinic, Tmmy's one year-old body failed him, and he slipped away in Jamie's arms.

It was only a few days later that Jamie asked if I would connect with Timmy for her. She was feeling guilty, and blamed herself for his sudden demise.

"I should have taken him in sooner," she agonized.

Jamie's pain was obvious as I drew Timmy's energy to me. He sent his love right away.

"From the heart of my soul," he said as he came through, vibrant and glowing. He showed me a brilliant light that was shining on him, and said that it felt really good, "better than sunshine."

Timmy showed me that he was surrounded with joy and laughter, and that he was in a place of celebration.

Timmy went on to describe his purpose in life with Jamie, and how his suffering on Earth had earned him a special kind of privilege.

"A joyous movement occurred when I transitioned," he explained, "A celebration of life, not of death. It moved me closer to the Eternal One, the One Being of Light our Creator, the Divine."

Then Timmy described how his soul evolved to the highest level, that of the Divine Masters.

"I am of that realm now," he stated. "All the events of my life are now understood, all meaningful. Now I can give back wisdom, knowledge, soul growth, peace, tranquility…everything a person yearns for. Tell mom not to be sad. Her life will be richer because of this. I see it on the higher plane, from a higher viewpoint. We couldn't have progressed any more, we limited out. I will bring others in who need you."

In closing, Timmy told Jamie to stay connected with him through prayer and mediation, then he pulled his energy away. It was hardly a day later when Serengeti entered Jamie's life. Serengeti was born with Manx Syndrome. The gene causes

Serengeti

spinal defects and can be fatal, but Serengeti is dealing well with her disability.

Serengeti is a happy little girl, full of energy. She doesn't know that she has a disability. She gets around well and likes to play with her new friends. She loves people and especially loves her new mom, Jamie.

Visualization and Prayer for Release

If animals are still emotionally attached to us at the time of their passing, it's possible they will hold on to the Earth plane, unable to continue their journey. Some animals will hold on because they don't want to upset us or cause us pain.

It's always best to give our animal companions permission to continue their journey into the spirit world so they may continue their spiritual journey back home to their Creator and Infinite Love.

Visualize your animal being surrounded by glorious angels as you say this prayer. Imagine their wings, spreading wide to surround the animal with loving warmth and wrap them in their ever-loving beauty. Imagine the glow as the angels comfort and calm your animal.

A simple prayer will help animals release their ties to the Earth and set them free to continue their journeys. Any prayer you feel comfortable with may be used, but this is one of my favorites:

I call upon the angels of love and mercy and ask them to surround (name the animal), who has passed into spirit but holds on to Earthly ties. I ask that you allow (name the animal) to release the bonds that hold (him or her) and give (him or her) wings to fly into the heavens. Surround (him or her) with your love and warmth, and comfort (him or her) on the journey. I give (name the animal) permission to continue on the path to Glory and the Divine. Amen.

11
Unexpected
Visitors

Elke

Many times, the animals will bring other energies through during a session, much as in a long-awaited family reunion. I tell my clients that we never know what may come through during a session. If there's a message out there that you're supposed to receive, this may just be the time, as many souls see this as their opportunity to come through.

Denise and I met in Spokane when I connected with her yellow lab, Elke. It was during a session with her cat, Buffo, that Denise and I were very surprised by who decided to come through. This was a first for me and for Denise.

Buffo was originally named Buffy by Denise's parents. When they discovered that Buffy was a boy kitty, they decided that Buffo sounded more masculine.

Denise wanted me to connect with Buffo because she was worried about him. When Denise's parents passed, Buffo came to live with Denise and Elke. While Denise loves Buffo, she is a self-admitted "dog person." Denise wanted me to check in with Buffo to make sure he was happy because Denise's parents had adored him.

When I connected with Buffo, he was easy going and very much okay. He told me how he was content with his life and really didn't need Denise to do anything different for him.

When Denise asked him if he missed her mom and dad, Buffo replied, "Well, of course not. They're right here."

At that moment, I felt two other energies enter my space. This had never happened before. I specifically felt the parents' energy come through, almost like Johnny Carson coming through that stage curtain on the old *Tonight Show*!

The energy from the parents was very loving toward their daughter and Buffo, who took a back seat while I opened up the channel to communicate with Denise's parents. Both her mom and dad came through with messages of love for Denise, and gratitude toward her for taking such good care of Buffo, "dog person" or not!

Although their messages were difficult to translate, I was able to pinpoint specific messages from mom and dad that only Denise knew to be true. It was a joyous moment for all of us.

After they sent their love and I felt their energies pull away, Denise and I were both speechless. Buffo, on the other hand, still had a lot to say! He felt very proud of himself for bringing mom and dad through.

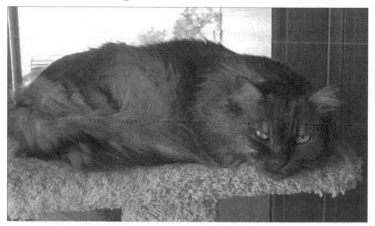

Buffo

Denise's parents continued to manifest during my ensuing sessions with her. At another Spokane event, Denise's mom came through and showed me Denise standing in her kitchen, "filling up a jar or container of some sort."

When I told this to Denise, she gasped with a big smile and said, "Just this morning I was in my kitchen filling up the cookie jar! Mom must have been there too!"

Denise's dad would not be left out of the action. He came through to me with a reference about Denise's front porch.

"Denise, are you doing some work on your front porch?" I asked her.

"Well, yes, my husband is repainting it this weekend. Why do you ask?"

"Because your dad is here, and he's telling me he sees this and he likes the color!"

It's always a pleasure for me to be a part of these reunions. Many times, the messages will be about simple things or events in life, so people know it was meant just for them.

Denise's parents grabbed the chance to come through, realizing that I would let her know that they were still part of her life and that they saw the ordinary things she did from day to day.

An Apology from the Spirit World

I'm often asked if I do readings for people. I usually answer that I only do readings for the animals, but the true answer is "yes." I connect with the animals first. The animals can bring other energies through during a session, from deceased human loved ones, spirit guides, angels or deceased animal loved ones.

If there's a message that someone wants to give you, they see a session with me as an opportunity to do so. I'll sometimes be right in the middle of a session when the messages just stop making sense. I've learned that this is usually another energy trying to get my attention and come through with messages for the human.

In one memorable session, a deceased mother came through with a long overdue apology for her unsuspecting daughter.

Janice and her mom, Kathy, came to see me in Spokane at a holistic event. The session started out centered on Janice's little dog, Star. Star was having some behavior problems, and I was helping Janice figure out what was going on. As I focused in on Star's energy, I felt another energy enter my space and come through.

This feels very much like when you're in line at the grocery store and someone walks up behind you. It isn't necessary to turn around to see him or her, but you can feel the presence. This is because the person has entered into your aura, a field of energy that surrounds our bodies. This auric field changes shape and color as our moods change throughout the day. If we're not feeling well or are overly stressed, our auras tend to be smaller and darker in color. When we're happy, our auras are larger and more colorful. Many can see auras, including children and animals.

I've had many clients report to me that their animals are looking up at the ceiling, toward a blank wall, or staring at one spot for an unusually long period. Not to worry. It's probably just a deceased loved one checking in on you or an angel stopping by for a visit.

When I sense an energy coming through during a session, I immediately see their auric field, their energy. They can appear with colors in an abstract shape, or they can be very dim and very dark.

The energy that was coming through during Janice's session revealed to me that she was "mom," a female energy. This presence was surrounding Janice's mom, Kathy.

I said, "Perhaps I have Kathy's mom here." Kathy gasped in surprise and got very still.

The messages that started to come through told a story of a very troubled relationship. Kathy's mother, Judy, had passed more than ten years before, and they had never become close. The spirit energy told me to please ask for her daughter's forgiveness, and showed me that she had not been very kind to her daughter during her life on Earth. She expressed her love for her daughter and apologized for her inappropriate behavior. This apologetic soul hoped that her estranged daughter would be able to open her heart and forgive her.

Kathy sat silently, listening to the messages. There was no response at all.

Janice had tears in her eyes as they thanked me and said goodbye when the session ended.

About a week later, Janice sent me this letter:

Dear Karen,

I just wanted to say "Thank You" for your reading this past Saturday at the "Body, Mind, and Spirit" Expo. More than what you said about our pets was what you told my mom about the "presence" around her (which was probably her mom.) Without going into any detail of her childhood, it is fair to say that my mom was not raised in a loving, healthy home.

Letting her know that my grandmother was sorry, loved her, and wanted forgiveness was a truly amazing thing to hear. I know that it will take my mom a little time for it sink in, but I feel so good about her hearing that, and I think my mom does too. After my grandma passed, I heard her clearly say, "I'm sorry, I never meant to hurt anyone," but I don't believe at the time my mom was ready to accept it.

It's been many years since she died, and I think my mom was ready, and more importantly, needed, to hear what you told her. Thank you, that was a wonderful gift and I wanted you to know I appreciated you sharing what you saw and heard more than I can describe.

Thank you,
Janice

Unresolved feelings between loved ones sometimes carry over into the spirit realms. Make your peace now, while you are still able to. Forgiveness is for you, not for the person you are forgiving. Their actions are not being erased or forgotten, but we can move forward and heal those old wounds.

In this line of work, I'm lucky enough to meet some of the nicest, kindest, most loving people imaginable. Some are what I call true animal lovers, devoted to rescuing or fostering animals in need. Two of these wonderful people came to me when health issues were affecting their dogs.

Scooter and Bebe

I met Bob and Valerie during a session with their two silky terriers, Scooter and Bebe. Scooter was very ill and Bob and Val wanted to know if he was ready to transition into the spirit world. All I knew at the beginning of this session was Scooter's name, age and that he wasn't doing very well.

Scooter delivered many loving messages, including how "heart-

Scooter

broken" he was for putting his mom and dad through so much turmoil. Scooter's voice was very clear.

"I've been trying to hold it together, but I can't hold on much longer."

The pain and discomfort was too intense for his little body.

"He talks about being out of his body a few times. The level of pain and discomfort is to the point where it's easier for him to not be in his body," I explained to Bob and Val. "I see him coming out of his body a few times. The pain is too hard for him to bear."

Humans and animals both have the ability to leave their bodies and experience what's called astral travel or astral projection. Astral projection is an interpretation of an out-of-body experience achieved either awake or through deep meditation or lucid dreaming. People who say they've experienced astral projection often claim that their consciousness or soul has transferred into an astral body or body-double, which moves in tandem with the physical body in a parallel world known as the astral plane.

The concept of astral projection has been around for thousands of years, dating back to ancient China. It is currently associated with the New Age movement. It's believed that the soul stays connected with the physical body through a "silver cord" but can rise up and lift itself into other realms. Once this silver cord is disconnected, the soul leaves the physical body and begins its transition into spirit realms.

Val confirmed that Scooter was on pain medication, but it wasn't really helping at that point. When Bob asked Scooter about the pain in his head, he described a "wincing type of thing. It feels like a piercing in my head; it makes me wince."

Val confirmed that Scooter suffered from a form of encephalitis, an inflammation of the brain usually caused by a viral infection or a hypersensitivity reaction to a virus or foreign protein. The inflammation is a reaction of the body's immune system to infection or invasion. During the inflammation, the brain's tissues become swollen. The combination of the infection and the immune reaction to it can cause headache and a fever, as well as more severe symptoms in some cases.

Scooter showed me he wanted his mom and dad to know how grateful he was for all they had done for him.

"Mom and dad, I love you so much. This has been a wonderful life with you, (even with the) odds stacked against me, here I am all because of you. Thank you for this. (I am) forever grateful, and (you will) always be in my heart."

Val confirmed that Scooter had many other health issues, calling him her "miracle child."

"He wasn't supposed to be born," Val explained. "He broke his back and wasn't supposed to walk again, he's a miracle."

Scooter explained how he very much wanted his legacy to continue, to help others with medical issues so they could enjoy a happy and loving family. Even though Scooter's prognosis was terminal, Bob and Val were able to ask him what his final wishes were and to send him all of their love.

We've also had many sessions with Bebe, Bob and Val's other silky, who has had her share of medical issues as well. It's always helpful to know exactly where an animal is feeling pain so you and your veterinarian can assess a treatment and recovery plan. Bob and Val go beyond the call of duty in making sure their animals' wishes are met. I'm honored and blessed to call them my friends. Here's a letter they sent me:

Dear Karen,

What a wonderful gift you have. It is because of you that Valerie and I were able to let our little Scootie know how much we loved him before he crossed over. You were right in tune with him and the messages you relayed from him were right on target, even the pictures you presented to us were Scootie. You were able to tell how he was feeling and communicate how much he loved us and relay how much we loved him. We were able to be there for him during his last days and knew when it was time for him to be able to move on.

You have been with us for our little BeBe, keeping us informed of how she has been feeling and what she needs from us during her illness. The messages you have communicated to us have been right on the mark and it is so valuable to hear exactly what BeBe is saying. Good or bad you let our little girl speak.

Valerie and I both highly recommend Karen, a talented and compassionate communicator, to others who want to get in tune with their pet and know exactly what is going on in their minds and spirit, and so we would recommend her to anyone who is thinking of using a communicator for the first time.

Many blessings to you,
Bob & Val

Bebe

Spirit Guides

I always say that if there's a message that you need to hear, the Universe will find some way to deliver it to you.

It was just this kind of message that came through for Carla during a psychic fair in Spokane. Originally, Carla came to see me for a session for her many beloved animals, some living and some in the spirit world. One of the sessions with Carla took even me by surprise. I've had many unexpected visitors appear during a session, but this one was really unique!.

I was connecting with Takoda, Carla's male heeler. I recognized very quickly that Koda was an "old soul," very evolved

Takoda

and highly spiritual.   Almost immediately, Koda brought through these amazing energies. They swooped down from the upper corner of the hall and made their entrance known to me.

Three incredible spirit guides appeared before me. It was a phenomenal sight! They were vibrant, and expressed deep loving emotions. One carried a staff with a crystal-like globe on the top. The main guide spoke to me telepathically and told me they were "beings of light and messengers of wisdom and knowledge."

They wore red robes with gold trim that were flowing around them. Their energy glowed like a Christmas tree, white and vibrant. I knew this would bring an important message for Carla, so I listened very closely.

The leader explained to me that they were the "masters, there to bring messages to Carla." They saw this as their chance to come through for her, representing, "truth and honesty."

Carla sat with her eyes wide open, taking in all the information.

After the session, Carla and I were discussing what had just happened when I was compelled to do an "automatic writing" from the leader.

Automatic writing is the process, or product, of writing that does not come from the conscious thoughts of the writer. The writer's hand forms the message, and the person is unaware of what will be written. It is sometimes done in a trance state. At other times, the writer is aware (not in a trance) of his or her surroundings, but not of the actions of the writing hand.

Here is what I wrote:

We are the messengers of light.

We don't speak but we hear.

We don't feel but we sense.

We are the light within and the dimensions beyond.

We bring truth and bring peace to all who listen.

She is our catalyst.

The weaver of the future.

This incredible session has changed Carla's life completely. Here is Carla's experience in her own words.

I met Karen briefly in the spring of 2005. We chatted for a few minutes at her table, and I entered the drawing for a half price session.

A few months later, I received a postcard from Karen informing me that I won the drawing! I was excited but frustrated at the same time as I was flat broke at that moment. I tossed the postcard on my desk where it proceeded to get buried under layers of files and paper.

During the rest of the summer, I thought about that postcard frequently which led me on a reading binge of anything related to metaphysical or psychic studies. I have always been intrigued by this subject matter and felt especially drawn to a book about how to connect with your spirit guides.

It was now late fall, I was at my desk working with the television droning in the background. I wasn't really paying

*attention to it. I looked down at the top of my untidy desk and
noticed that Karen's postcard had mysteriously surfaced. It had
been months since I had seen it last.*

*I picked up the postcard and wondered if it was still valid. As
I pondered that question, a commercial came on for the local
psychic fair. As I looked up they announced the "Special guest
speaker, Karen Anderson, Animal Communicator." Okay, that
was it, I told myself. I have to call her.*

*I called Karen and set an appointment for mid afternoon at the
expo. I arrived early to wander around the venue and check out
the other vendors before my session. I was drawn to a particular
booth that had various tapes for sale. One tape caught my eye
and I picked it up. It was about uniting with an ancient spirit
guide I excitedly purchased the tape, put it in my backpack and
headed over to Karen's booth.*

*Karen had no idea about my earlier reading binge about spirit
guides or that I had just moments earlier purchased a cassette
tape on the topic. The session I had with her left me completely
stunned. I sat there in awe and admittedly a bit frightened,
overwhelmed by what had just happened. My dog, Takoda
brought three of my spirit guides through during the session.*

*I sat there reeling, trying to make sense of it all when I
remembered the tape I just purchased. I pulled the cassette from
my backpack and showed it to Karen.*
She looked at the tape and shook her head, smiling.

*"When Spirit has a message for you they find a way to deliver
it," she said knowingly. "They saw the opportunity to come
through to me during your session. This is awesome!"*

*That incredible event was the beginning of a brand new
chapter in my life. My spiritual awakening unfolded before my
own eyes. I felt like I had finally found the right path in my life.
Since that pivotal day, amazing things have happened. Studying
under Karen, I have learned how to communicate with animals
and I have also connected with my own guides, and now I hear
their messages. I have manifested the most incredible people
into my life and I owe it all to Karen for opening the door for*

me. She is my mentor and friend. Without her none of this would have been possible.
Thank you, Karen!

Love & Light, Carla

Pink roses

I was in session with Patty and her cat, Abigail, discussing some medical issues that were causing Abigail to lose weight. After we resolved the weight-loss problem, Abigail suddenly brought another energy through.

I told Patty that we had an unexpected visitor, a female energy that was saying "mom" to me.

"Tell her mom," the energy prompted me.

Patty was beside herself with excitement, exhilaration and sadness all at once. Her mother had passed just three months earlier. Patty had been very close to her mom, and this unexpected chance to hear her mom's messages was bittersweet. Patty's mom came through with gentle guidance for Patty, urging her to stay true to her life's dream of working with children with special needs. She also reassured Patty that she would always stay connected with her, even from the other side. At the end of the session, Patty's mom showed me a bouquet of pink roses.

Patty was overjoyed: Pink roses were her mother's favorite flowers!

12
Final Thoughts

The author and a friend in the 1970s

As I look back at all the sessions I've had with animals over the years, I realize that not a single animal has ever refused to communicate with me. Oh sure, some have been more outgoing than others, and some have chosen not to discuss painful or difficult experiences, but I honor their wishes and respect their boundaries.

I've found that coming from the heart with loving thoughts, telling them how handsome they are or how gorgeous they are, is a wonderful way to begin a communication session.

A client of mine in the Sacramento, California, area reported to me that her lost cat, Saki, would only answer to me after several others attempted to communicate with him. I believe this is because of the gentle and loving approach I try to take, and my deep respect for those animals with whom I connect. I truly love animals to the core of my being. They can sense this, and they can tell what our intentions are.

Their personalities are as different and varied as our own. They are very much like us in many ways and yet so different. Remember, they are animals, with instincts and behaviors that don't always fit into our modern lives.

Being open to their perspectives and understanding their wishes can work wonders on resolving conflicts. Patience and perseverance are also required, but most issues can be resolved to bring about more balance and harmony for everyone.

As their guardians, we provide food, water, shelter and love. We cannot however, control our companion animal's destiny, and when it's his or her time to pass into the spirit world, the best thing we can do is "fill the tank" with loving thoughts.

The animals have told me that, when we grieve for them, our guilt, sorrow and emotional ties drain them of their energy, leaving them "on empty," so to speak, for the long journey ahead.

We need to "fill them up." You would never think of going on a vacation without first stopping by the gas station and topping off the tank. Your loving thoughts and prayers are the fuel. Their

hearts are the tank. Think about the happy times, the things they did to make you laugh, the joy they brought to you.
Those thoughts will fill their tanks to overflowing.

Think of their passing into the spirit world as though they were going on a very long vacation, a journey that may take them right back into your arms. The sooner you can fill them up and send them on their way, the sooner they can return to you for another enchanted lifetime.

Cherish them while they are here, honor them and say their names often when they have passed on. Even the challenges they bring us are to help us learn and grow as spiritual beings ourselves.

I've learned many valuable lessons from the animals. I take better care of myself and try to live each day to the fullest. I know that each day is a blessing and each moment we have with our animal companions is a gift. I've learned to listen to what my heart tells me but, no matter what, to follow the path I was destined for.

I look forward to having many more conversations with the animals, as this is just the beginning.

As Noah the dove so eloquently said, "You are a child of God. You know in your heart that you must continue your work. Fear not, my child, it is your purpose in this lifetime."

The Author

Karen Anderson, "America's Animal Communicator," has studied under some of the world's most renowned psychics. Karen's abilities allow her to connect with animals both living or deceased, bringing messages of love, forgiveness and much needed healing to aching hearts. Devoted to the animals since childhood, Karen's abilities began during her younger years when she thought everyone

Photo by Myron G. Bursell

could talk to the animals. Then a sudden and tragic accident caused her to shut down her abilities, or so she thought.... Her calling to work with the animals returned again as an adult, and now Karen travels the world lecturing, teaching workshops and sharing her love of all animals. Karen lives and works in Elk, Washington, where she continues to be a voice and an advocate for all creatures.

This is her first book.

Acknowledgments

There are many people I need to acknowledge for their support and encouragement in the writing of this book. My husband, Daniel, for always being there for me: Thank you from the depths of my soul. To my Ursula and Tony, my mom and dad, for allowing me to have animals in my life while I was growing up.

To my sister, Kathi: Thank you for proofreading! To my aunt Renate for helping with the title; and the rest of my family: Thank you for your love and support.

To my dear friends, whom I can always count on: Cathy Valigura, Carla Haley and Shelly Christensen, thank you. To the special clients and friends whose stories are chronicled in this book, thank you for sharing your most precious moments with all of us.

A special thank you to Dannion Brinkley, whose insight inspired me to write this book. Also for reminding me that my work will not only help humans and animals understand each other better, it will also allow us to move past our fear of the afterlife.

Another special thank you goes to Rich Hopkins, who really hounded me (no pun intended) to get the manuscript done.

An extra special thank you to Linda Lael Miller, who miraculously entered my life right when I needed her the most. I will be forever grateful and thankful to all of you!

To my agent, Antoinette Kuritz, for making this happen, and to the entire staff at New River Press, I am so grateful to all of you.

Finally, I need to thank the animals, angels and spirit guides in my life for assisting me on my journey, being there during those difficult times and creating true joy in my life. Without all of you, I never would have taken this path.